I0790542

DYNAMIC LEADERSHIP

A Visionary Leader That Changes the World

ZAHID KHAN

authorHOUSE®

AuthorHouse™ UK
1663 Liberty Drive
Bloomington, IN 47403 USA
www.authorhouse.co.uk
Phone: UK TFN: 0800 0148641 (Toll Free inside the UK)
*   UK Local: 02036 956322 (+44 20 3695 6322 from outside the UK)*

Published by AuthorHouse   06/03/2021

ISBN: 978-1-6655-8314-5 (sc)
ISBN: 978-1-6655-8313-8 (e)

Print information available on the last page.

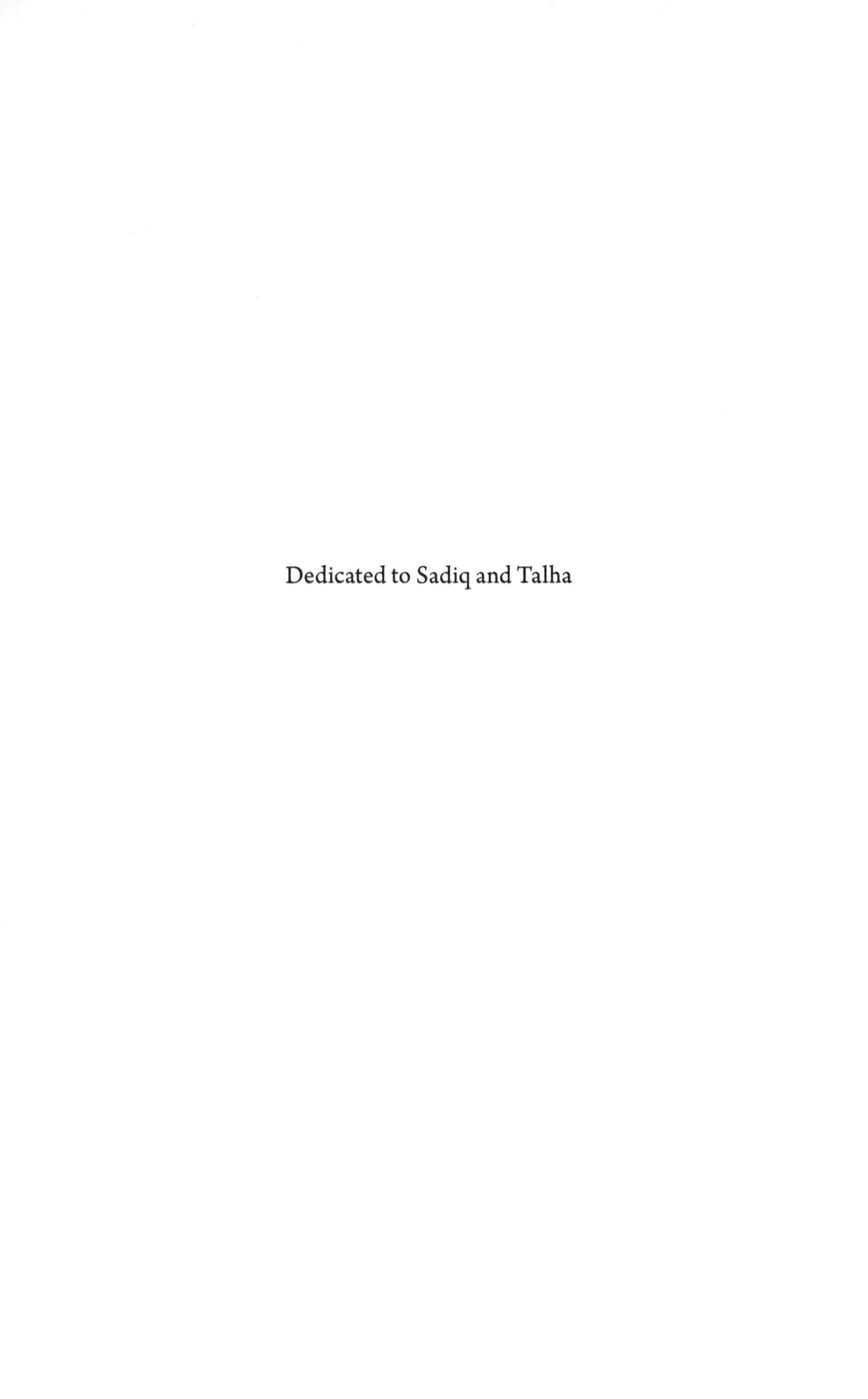

Dedicated to Sadiq and Talha

CONTENTS

CHAPTER 1

Introduction

THE HISTORY OF LEADERSHIP IS as old as history itself. The relation between leader and follower starts from the day human beings came to this world. Humans considered it a necessity to be led by an experienced person for their affairs and social life.

Many books have been written about leadership, but still, I felt a vacuum and realized that a book needs to be written from a different perspective. After all, the welfare, prosperity, and development of a nation depend on the capability and vision of their leaders. The more efficient and visionary a leader is, the more the nation will advance in all spheres of life. This book is mainly about the ethics and integrity of a leader. These are the foremost qualities of leaders that make them stand out. Before anything else, leaders need the trust of their followers to maintain relations. Leaders have to be trustworthy, and they have to do what they say.

I am referring to the leaders who are loved by their followers and are capable of leading. They are models, they take the initiative, and they not only listen to people but also act and solve their problems. They are dynamic, active, charismatic and proactive. They have to be aware of the environment and keep themselves updated on all developments around them; they must be competent in their job.

We expect that leaders will take care of their followers, listen to individuals, and find solutions for their problems. Those leaders who treat people fairly are successful. History remembers those who are fair to their people and who give vision to a country, community, or organization. Leaders have to see everything themselves and do not merely depend on people's feedback.

This book is as important for experienced organizational leaders as it is for leadership students and others. In today's world, leaders are not just politicians, but everyone who runs an organization, a small business, or a community group is known as a leader. Fairness is an important quality in a leader. In any organization, fairness is of paramount importance. An organization will fail if the people see the leader as unfair. Failure will not come overnight; it may take years. A leader has to have a vision for the organization, transmit it to others, and get their commitment. Leaders must not keep power to themselves; they must delegate it and make sure that others are transparent and fair. If leaders of the organizations are fair but the people they delegate power to are not, the result is the same as if the leaders themselves are unfair. A leader has to make sure that others have the same values. Many times, people suffer not because of the CEO but because of a poor divisional or unit leader.

This book is important for students as well as for others. Students are an important portion of our society; they are tomorrow's leaders. Students have to learn the skills of leading, speaking, managing, and coaching. They have to develop the values of integrity, fairness, and ethics, and bring these qualities to the organizations, communities, and governments. Today's world is a global village, and business schools and universities have to teach skills that are compatible with multiple cultures. Whether you are in DR Congo, Indonesia, Singapore, Boston, New York, or Riyadh, you need the skills required to run the organization in the environment where you work. People all over the world want to be treated well and respected, and they also expect this for others.

I am writing this book for all those categories. I hope that everyone will take advantage of reading the book and make comments.

Qualities of a Leader

Leaders are people who lead a group, an organization, a community, or a country. Leaders give vision to a group, organization, or country; set goals; and get the commitment of people to achieve the goals. Leaders are aware of the environment in which the organization works and keep the organization updated as changes occur. Nowadays, one constant thing is change. Leaders dream for the future, give the organization a long-term vision, and want the organization to reach that vision within a specific time period. Leaders transmit the vision to the people and inspire them, providing them all resources necessary to reach the targeted goals.

Leaders are examples of morality and have high integrity. They sacrifice their time to serve the people. They say what they mean and mean what they say, and are always at disposal of the people. Their values make them valuable to the people. They trust the people and don't monitor them all the time. They take responsibility for all their actions, accept their mistakes, and correct themselves. They get feedback from everyone and see themselves in the eyes of the people. They are aware of skilled people and use them to their potential. They get advice from people and encourage them to participate in the discussion.

Leaders are role models; those who are charming behave and act towards people in a certain way. They create an environment where everyone is happy, and people love their job. They help people to achieve their goals, encourage them to take the initiative, and respect people who work hard and are outstanding performers. Leaders mirror the characteristics of a group and view their staff the way they see themselves. Leaders protect their staff, and there is an environment of trust around. Leaders with good morals win the people.

On the other hand, when leaders are on the defensive, they will hardly create an environment of trust, and no one will feel secure. People will consume their energy to protect themselves. Their full energy will not go to achieving organizational goals. All organizations and communities need leaders who are models for everyone. Apart from other skills, they have to have integrity and believe in equality for everyone. They must dedicate their full energy to the organization's business and not work on their personal agenda.

Leaders have different styles, and different leaders act differently on different occasions. To be popular, leaders have to take care of their people, meet them, and listen to their concerns; they try their best to find solutions. People expect that they will be heard by their leaders. National or party leaders have to act according to people's expectations. They have to pull them out from economic problems. Leaders have to be good speakers and communicators. They must be reachable and live a simple life. They must avoid nepotism or favouritism, which is the root of all problems. They avoid personal desires. They are totally selfless. They have to have a mission for which they struggle. As Nelson Mandela said, "A leader without a mission is not a leader." Leaders should have discipline, commitment, and determination.

Individuals are members of any organization, community, or country who follow the leader. In today's world, there is big competition in all walks of life, and to be successful and survive, you need a strong leader. Any group, organization, or country needs a strong leader for its existence. The viability of any organization depends on its leader's vision. Leaders give direction to people and get their commitment to contribute to achieving future goals and dreams. Leaders shape the organization's future and give it a long-terms strategy. The job of a leaders is not easy. They must inspire the people, lead the organization, and often manage big projects.

How to Become a Leader

Some believe that leaders are born with charismatic personalities that help them influence people. I don't agree with that; leadership skills can be learned, and anyone can become a leader. You have to know what the skills of the leader are and how to learn them.

I am writing this book to stress the effective qualities of a dynamic leader that are key for the success of an organization, country, or community. This book is about leadership in a broad sense. Although I have addressed leaders in an organization and their key qualities, the emphasis of this book is global leaders who get the commitment of the people by virtue of their honesty, morality, and integrity.

The rise and fall of a nation depend on the capabilities of its leader. An ethical and competent leader will pull people out from a miserable life into a successful and happy one. Leaders with strong values and vision will shake the nation. They will guide the people to realize their vision into reality, which will change their lives. In subsequent chapters, I explain how leaders should be.

In chapter 2, I discuss a leader's vision. Visionary leaders are future-oriented and have a picture in mind for the organization, country, or community that promises a better change. They share that vision with the organization, community, or country to have a better life in future. They are not happy with the status quo and want to change it. They get others to commit to achieving their corporate goals. They create a culture where everyone is motivated to work hard. There is a team spirit, and people work in cohesion, with common values and goals. They move in the same direction, with the same destination. The vision and dream of the leader is so powerful that it attracts everyone. It is a promise for a better future. These leaders are concerned about outcomes, not activities. Visionary leaders can bring about changes in the lives of their followers. They are well informed and keep the country, organization, or community moving in the right direction. They also formulate a strategy to realize their vision. Their vision exists in the future, but their present concern is to create a culture of collaboration, teamwork, flexibility, communication, and empathy. Their followers feel honoured to work with them.

Chapter 3 is about the art of communication. I call it an art, as you have to decorate your message like an artist adds colour to a design. Communication plays an important role in a leader's mission. I have emphasized that leaders are good communicators and convey their vision, objectives, and goals through various channels. They promote communication and encourage others to share information and knowledge. They inform their followers whenever decisions are made. They take them into confidence about any changes. They communicate in writing but are also verbally eloquent. They use gestures and positive body language to communicate. Communication is a powerful tool if used properly. With their communication skills, leaders update the people working with them.

In chapter 4, I discuss how leaders delegate authority and tasks to others. Leaders may be overwhelmed with their tasks. They have to think about their vision, strategy, and objectives. They have to think about the organization's competitors. If you are in politics, your competitors will be other political parties. If you lead a company, other businesses are your competitors. You have to delegate some of your tasks to your subordinates and allocate your time to the organization's strategy and objectives. Delegation is not easy; leaders have to know how to do it.

Delegation includes responsibility, authority, and accountability. You have to choose people who are competent and capable of doing the job. There must be mutual trust between the two. You have to inform them why they were chosen for the task, describe how significant the assignment is for the organization, and explain how it will make a difference. If they accept it, leaders must take their workload into consideration. There must be a balanced approach. Delegatees have to be trained and briefed about expected results. The emphasis should be on the outcome and desired results.

The delegation of authority should be formally documented. There must be a system that monitors delegatees periodically. Delegators and delegatees should have a good relationship and communicate with each other on a regular basis. Delegatees should get feedback from delegator from time to time. Delegatees should know where to go when they need help. Delegating authority expedites some operations, reducing the time for authorization. It moves responsibility to someone who is an expert and close to the clients or customers. Delegation of authority develops staff and creates more leaders. When individuals are delegated authority, they are motivated to work independently. They exhibit more dedication, take responsibility and accountability, and consider the tasks their own. It creates mutual trust and enhances the relationship between managers and subordinates. With delegation, subordinates consider these jobs meaningful and are more productive and innovative. They can develop their skills with the challenge of new responsibilities and can be considered for promotion. Leaders who are poorly prepared cannot delegate. Lack of trust can also make it difficult. Bad governance can also hinder the delegation of authority. With the delegation of authority, organizations expand and become more competitive in the marketplace.

Chapter 5 is about self-awareness and self-discipline. Self-awareness is the key quality of great leaders. The dilemma with many leaders is, they are not self-aware. The Greek philosopher Socrates was asked to define wisdom. He said, "Know thyself." If you know yourself, your strengths and weaknesses, then you can work on them. You have to see yourself in the eyes of others. How is your image? How you are emotionally intelligent? Always monitor your emotions, your reaction in each situation. If you know it, then you can work on it and improve yourself.

For example, if there is a sudden accident, this is an opportunity to see your reactions and emotions at that moment. Get feedback from peers, colleagues, subordinates, and others, and continuously work on yourself. Your self-awareness should not be a perception of yourself but a reality. As Dr Tasha Eurich, a motivational speaker, says, "If you are more self-aware, you are more effective, promotable and more fulfilled." This is of paramount importance for a leader to be self-aware. People rarely give you feedback; it's your responsibility to work on yourself. The more you are self-aware, the more you will be successful.

Then comes self-discipline. The best leaders have self-discipline. Self-discipline is the bridge between goals and accomplishment. You have a purpose in life. You have goals and objectives. In order to achieve your goals, you impose some laws on yourself and work on your goals every day. This is the only thing that will lead you to your destination. Without discipline, you will not be able to control yourself. If you don't discipline yourself, you will go nowhere. Time or other people will control you. With self-discipline, you live your life on your terms. It narrows your focus and removes distractions and unnecessary things; you only work on your goals. This is the key for any successful leader.

Chapter 6 discusses the integrity, ethics, and values of a great leader. Integrity and ethical behaviour are of paramount importance for a leader. The focus of this book is on ethical leaders. All other qualities are necessary and contribute to your success, but ethics and integrity are fundamental and the most important. People with these qualities show ethical behaviour and principles. It is the basis for your relations with others.

Integrity is the only quality that will keep you ahead of others. You keep yourself correct and fulfil your promise. Your word is your bond. You mean what you say and say what you mean. With ethical behaviour, you become selfless and always prefer the interests of others. People feel easy working with you. They know you will be fair with them. Ethical leaders bring transparency to organizations. People are hired and promoted purely on merit basis. People love them with all their heart. As we see on a national level, ethical leaders get the commitment of the people. They bring a revolution into their lives. They are trusted for their decisions. People are well aware that whatever they do, they do for the people with sincerity.

On the international level, it is even more important to be ethically correct. Leaders are always watched and judged by the people. They have to be very careful when dealing with people. People will note every little thing they say or write. If leaders are selfless and have no interests and work for others, they have to make it known to the people. Ethical leaders will be popular among the people and can help a country to develop.

Chapter 7 discusses leaders as change agents. It's very important for leaders to be change agents. In today's volatile environment the only thing which is constant is change. If you don't change your organization with a changing world, you will lose your viability. You cannot work in a modern world with old technology. With technological development, technological systems are replaced every five years. Change is not only about operational improvement or process reengineering; it is also about radically changing organizational culture.

Being a change agent is very complex for leaders. They have to study the organization's culture, people's behaviour, procedures, guidelines, strategy, corporate objectives, and goals. They need good relations with internal players who run the business. They need to maintain good relations with them to get their commitment. They have to listen to everyone to see how the current system is. At times, an outsider change agent is hired and works with an internal change agent. A change agent should have the authority to bring about changes. This job needs patience, perseverance, and tolerance. Agents will face many obstacles, as people are reluctant to change. They have to convince them that it is for their betterment. They will have a better life after this change.

Chapter 8 is about training and continuous learning. Another important quality of great leaders is that they are lifelong learners. Leaders are readers and never stop learning. They learn new skills to cope with unexpected challenges. They learn from experience, setbacks, and failure. There is no better teacher than experience. They learn from every challenge. They go to training and take courses. Leaders also attend executive MBA programmes. They have to learn everything about their subject. They have to be very dynamic and keep an eye on the changing environment, political situation, and regulations. Leaders come to their position of leadership due to their learning. They not only learn themselves but also encourage others to learn and develop. The organization becomes a learning company, and everyone is motivated to learn.

With such a leader, you can climb the ladder and get a higher position. Learning produces more leaders and results in organizational development. Learning changes your behaviour. If you learn more, then you will never remain the same. You will see issues with a different view. Leaders allocate budget for learning, training, and career development. People are free to take courses and arrange for their learning. A learning organization is very effective and continuously expands. People become knowledgeable, which is an asset for the organization. Learning changes organizational culture. This chapter emphasizes that leaders should schedule a time for learning. Some leaders don't know what they don't know. Others know what they don't know. They arrange for their learning.

Chapter 9 discusses charismatic leaders. Charismatic leaders have charm and attract people with their charm. They inspire others with their charisma. They get commitments from others. Charismatic leaders are confident and under control. They don't micromanage. It is said that charisma is 50 per cent internal and 50 per cent external. Charismatic leaders are creative and innovative; they find new ways to achieve their goals. They have strong determination and good communication skills. They are persons of high integrity.

Chapter 10 discusses the key qualities of a transformational and model leader. I mention one example of model leaders. Although there are many, I have picked only one leader of recent history, Nelson Mandela. He was a model transformational leader who brought democracy to South Africa and treated everyone fairly after winning the election. He had patience, persistence, and perseverance. He is well respected throughout the world. He never gave up and continued his struggle till the end.

The difference between transformational and charismatic leaders is that charismatic leaders are concerned about the status quo, whereas transformational leaders make fundamental changes and transform the country, organization, or community. Every country is in dire need of a transformational leader to revolutionize their life.

Chapter 11 is about Covid-19, a challenge for leaders to address economic and health issues in a pandemic. After I finished the tenth chapter of my book, I decided to add another chapter on Covid-19, which has affected nearly every country in the world. Covid-19 is a new coronavirus that was reported in Wuhan, China, last year. Covid-19 is an infectious disease that can spread from person to person. It has spread all over the world. The symptoms can range from mild to severe illness. One can become infected by close contact with others. Old people are at high risk. Maintaining social distancing and staying at home are important to slow the spread of the disease; vaccines are being developed, but getting them to everyone in the world is a challenge.

The virus was limited to China, but as people travelled abroad, they took the virus with them, and the virus spread quickly. It has had a huge effect on business worldwide. This is a big challenge to governments, corporations, and organizations. Organizations have to reinvent themselves. People are forced to work from home. Although it has affected business tremendously, many organizations survived. The Internet has played a big role and facilitated the job of organizations, corporations, and government bodies.

Bibliography

Adair, J. (1998). *Effective Leadership: How to Develop Leadership Skills.* London: Macmillan.

Boutros-Ghali, B., et al. (1998). *Essays on Leadership.* New York: Carnegie Corporation.

Covey, S. R. (1992). *Principle-Centered Leadership.* New York: Simon & Schuster.

Covey, S. R. (2004). *The 7 Habits of Highly Effective People: Powerful Lessons in Personal Change. Restoring the Character Ethic.* New York: Simon & Schuster.

https://core.ac.uk/download/pdf/144980434.pdf.

https://www.econstor.eu/bitstream/10419/156751/1/17107-66665-1-PB.pdf. Accessed 23 Aug. 2020

https://www.enclaria.com/2019/02/05/seven-essential-traits-of-a-change-agent/. Accessed 23 Aug. 2020.

CHAPTER 2

A Leader's Vision

THE EXISTENCE OF ANY ORGANIZATION, corporation, or entity is the result of a leader's vision. Let us see first what vision is and how it is defined.

Vision can be defined as a picture in the leader's concept/imagination/ mind that inspires people to action when communicated compellingly, passionately, and clearly.

According to leadership guru Warren Bennis, "In order to take the organization to the highest possible level, leaders must engage their people with a compelling and tangible vision."

So vision is a key ingredient to a leader's mission and success.

A vision is a leader's dream about the future direction of the organization. The vision is shared across the organization, and people are emotionally committed to it. The leader imagines the vision as already achieved. It is very clear, and everyone understands it.

Leaders see their vision in the future; it exists in their imagination. Leaders give their vision to the organization as a goal. The leadership vision goes beyond a written mission statement. Unless leaders have a vision, they are not true leaders. They articulate their vision and values to the people. They create a culture in the organization where the people coherently act on their dreams.

Why is a vision necessary? Visions are needed when leaders are not happy with the status quo and want a change. They want to see the organization in a better situation in the future. So they share their dream, their vision, with the organization. Everything comes in imagination first, and then it comes into existence.

Good leaders share their vision clearly and set the organization's direction and purpose. They inspire the loyalty of the staff and create an environment of participation. Organizations are successful when their leader has a clear vision that's communicated to everyone with a compelling message. Leaders spend their time envisioning the future and enlisting help in achieving their dream. Boyd (1992a) suggests that a successful leader gives a widely shared sense of purpose or vision. A vision is a signpost pointing the way for all who need to understand what the organization is and where it intends to go (Nanus 1992). My understanding is that a vision should have a moral aspect that attracts the attention and commitment of workers and the general public. Visions are comprehensive; they are not only a dream of the future but also the means to accomplish it. They guide the work of the organization.

Seeley (1992) suggests that people's behaviour is guided by a goal-oriented mental construct. Leaders have to see the strength and weakness of the organization and convey their vision to all concerned. A culture of cooperation is created, and everyone is committed to the vision; good leaders inspire individuals to achieve targeted goals.

A vision gives you direction and eliminates any type of confusion. The most compelling vision attracts high commitment. It provides an excellent standard with ethical values. An organization without a vision perishes. The vision of the leader challenges the status quo and gives people hope for a new dawn. Their image connects you to the future.

As Michelangelo said, "The greater danger for most of us is not that our aim is too high and we miss it, but that it is too low and we reach it." A vision gives you discipline in life; every day you work on your vision and grow closer to achieving it. Visionary leaders are dynamic and future-oriented. They are not happy with the status quo, where people are unhappy. They are change agents and want to do things that improve the lives of others. People consider it an honour to work with visionary leaders who shake up the organization. An organization with a compelling vision attracts qualified people who can see a better future there.

Leaders with vision are optimistic and not pessimistic. Leaders with vision are always thinking and hoping for the future. They learn from failures and consistently work on their vision. They share their vision with others and accept suggestions from their team. They are very clear, and everyone is aware of their compelling vision. There is a coherent and concerted effort towards attaining their dreams. A vision without realization is not a vision. A vision doesn't remain only with the leader; it is publicized and spread through media and other sources. Organizations with effective leaders become known to everyone in the region. The general public and other organizations trust the compelling vision of their visionary leader. They want to engage with such an organization in order to get credibility. Other organizations copy it and follow their path in order to succeed and achieve their goals. It is an honour for staff to work in such an organization.

Visionary leaders think in a broad sense and are always concerned about the future. They provide a culture where people always think about improvement. We have seen leaders with big visions; history remembers those like Nelson Mandela of South Africa, who was jailed for twenty-seven years for his political beliefs but finally gained freedom for his people. His vision was equality in South Africa for everyone. He treated black and white people in the same way.

Leaders are able to translate their vision into reality. Leaders with a vision for a better future are loved by everyone. Visionary leaders are selfless and use their energy for the betterment of the people. They transform the lives of others and achieve big goals. History remembers those visionaries who left a legacy behind. Leader with a strong vision often think about people who are less fortunate and share their vision for a better future.

Visionary leaders not only change the life of the organization or community but also influence the general public. Their vision is accepted across the country. These visionaries are also examples of morality; they speak to the hearts of the people. People follow them willingly. Their vision is not the end of the game; they always have high goals. They take control of the organization and become models for others. Their competence, morality, and vision attract media attention. They are well known across the community, region, and country.

Organizations are viable when they have visionary leaders who shape the organization's future and give it a place and role in the market. The organization may be for profit or not for profit, it needs a leader who gives it direction and guidance where to go. Entrepreneurs first imagine a business in their mind and then establish the business to realize their vision. They move from small businesses to big ones and occupy a larger share of the market. If we take the example of the airplane, it was first imagined by its inventor and then came into existence. Marconi first imagined a radio and then made it. Vision and imagination are the keys to achieving any goal. How it may be, it is first imagined in the mind and then acted upon.

Leaders share their vision for a big dream, which seems impossible, but they make it happen. No matter what it takes, they achieve it. They are very consistent and committed, and they become role models. They work from dawn to dusk with passion. People are energized by seeing leaders as role models. People work on teams and contribute to achieving the goals of the organization. Visionary leaders sacrifice their interests for the interests of the community, organization, or country. They want to see the people happy. They study the status quo and plan how to go out of such a situation with a clear vision. They make all their efforts consistently and patiently to translate their vision into reality. They do it with the help of friends, colleagues, and other leaders.

Visionary leaders find ways to achieve their dreams and goals. They are well disciplined and manage their time wisely. They don't waste time on unnecessary things and prioritize their tasks. They produce highly productive teams who work smart. Their vision is on everyone's mind, and they find ways to realize it. These leaders think about the outcome and what they need to do. They rarely worry about activities. The picture of the outcome desired by the leader is on the mind of all managers, who plan their days to reach the outcome. Every day there is a step forward, and progress is visible and tangible. People dedicate their time and efforts to achieve the desired results.

Visionary leaders are challenging. Their vision is powerful and in line with the organization's culture, processes, and systems. It is stable, it is sustained over time, and it has a long-term perspective There is a continuous and consistent effort to realize the vision. People are empowered to get there. This vision gives people a clear picture of the future. Visionary leaders transform the organization and produce new leaders who continuously develop others to become leaders. Negative attitudes don't exist, and the organization is continuously on the path to success.

Everything ever invented on the earth was first imagined before it existed. For any success, you have to become visionary and see it in your mind first and continuously work on it in order to see it in real life. Visionary leaders are always in search of change; they concentrate on the outcome and find ways to get the desired result. Visionary leaders give purpose to an organization, community, or country. They think about why we do what we do.

A strong vision keeps people motivated, whatever the circumstances are. People enjoy their job and are motivated by an inspiring and powerful vision. Leaders who are self-disciplined share their effective vision and attract more customers. In such organizations, jobs are secure, and employees work hard. The organization develops and expands, and the number of staff and stakeholders increase. People are willing to invest in such organizations where they see a value for their investment. Qualified people apply for jobs where they see their future.

Banks and suppliers establish a relationship with such organizations for their growth and credibility. They use such organizations as references. Visionary leaders not only develop the organization and give it stature but also help employees to realize their dreams. Leaders take the ideas of others and prepare a shared vision that is acceptable to everyone and is in line with the organization's culture. They have big dreams for a vivid future. In order to realize their big dreams, they set small, short-term goals. These goals are tangible and are in line with the big dream.

Visionary leaders always think abstractly and are always in search of excellence. They want to serve others. Visionary leaders are always accessible and ready to meet the needs of others. In order to get excellence, they sacrifice their time, resources, and energy. They have high integrity and never misuse their resources.

I would emphasize you never use your office to support or help your friends or oppose your enemies, always be fair with everyone in the best interest of the organization/entity where you work. Dynamic and visionary leaders follow this path. There are shortcomings in organization, ministries, private sector where weak leaders use the office for friends which lead to nepotism and misuse of the resources.

Real leaders always think about official business. Visionary leaders are innovative and find novel solutions for problems. Leaders of an organization, community or country must be fair, impartial, honest, and flexible, and they must have an outstanding character. They are always concerned about the development and advancement of the people. They help vulnerable people and envision novel ideas to pull people out of a miserable status; they use all their efforts to improve their lives. They are in the hearts of the people. They sacrifice their time, energy, and money for the service of others. They are not selfish. They consider accountability.

Leaders with the qualities of discipline, ethics, enthusiasm, and charisma stand out to be the best leaders. Leaders lead by example. Dreams that are big can be achieved after a period of time. Some argue that a dream is not a picture but a movie in the future, and thousands benefit from it. The fundamental characteristic of a dream or vision has to be realistic, achievable, and tangible. Nothing is impossible if you work honestly with your heart, spirit, and brain, and use all your resources to achieve it. Masses can change the fate of the country if inspired by a dynamic leader.

In order to transform a country, leaders approach individuals, speak in public, write books, and use media to connect to the audience for a big breakthrough. In order to lead a country, you have to be visionary, honest, charismatic, and a good speaker. Leaders with a big mission can change history. They use the masses to achieve their collective goal. The leader's dream is the dream of the nation. Everyone makes an effort and uses their energy to realize the dream.

Visions lead to the success and viability of the organization, community, or country. Visions motivate people to move forward, despite all obstacles. Leaders believe that obstacles can't obstruct you, but they instruct you to move forward. Visionary leaders believe in success and strive to succeed without stopping. Their goal is on their mind, and all their efforts are concentrated on achieving the dream. They always think about the outcome and keep it in mind. They base their activities on the outcome. The organization has a purpose, and good leaders encourage innovation.

As Einstein said, "There is no limitation to imagination. You can go anywhere in imagination." First, people imagine a goal and then plan how to achieve it and then take action. A vision has to be very broad and based on knowledge and experience. Leaders are continuously learning and training. Leaders are readers. They are aware of the market situation. Their vision takes the organization from poor performance to the highest level. Visions have no limitations, and a strong and effective vision can change the fate of a nation. It gives you momentum in a forward direction. Visionary leaders don't keep you in a static position; they always give you the momentum to move forward and change.

Every big company is the result of the vision of its leader, who first imagined it and then inspired people to make that dream a reality. Landing on the moon was the vision of a leader. Visions motivate and inspire people to move forward. Powerful visions will get the commitment of many people. Visionary leaders are risk-takers. Visionary leaders boldly take risks and get the commitment of others. They share the vision for the betterment of the people. They create teams of committed people.

Visionary leaders are emotionally intelligent and self-aware. They have empathy for others and respond positively to people's emotions. They are sympathetic and sociable. They listen to others and don't turn a deaf ear to their opinions. They are like servants of their followers and work day and night for their betterment. Their integrity and ethics are well known, and no one can question their honesty and fairness.

They keep themselves well informed of the changing world and respond effectively to changes and new developments. They have strong values and transfer those values to others. Because of their strong and compelling vision, people perform well. As a result, the organization stands out. Their vision clearly defines how the future could be. They encourage learning and training for their people. They also have lifelong learning goals. They never stop learning and always try to learn new skills. They think strategically and prepare a powerful strategy for the organization. They create a road map for the organization to achieve its goals. They create an environment of collaboration and trust. They enhance the morale of followers and pull them out of hopelessness.

Visionary leaders can change the world. They bring revolution into the lives of the people. They change their perception and make the impossible possible. The fate of the people depends upon the vision of the leader. People want change to have a better life. Visionary leaders guide them to this change. They need someone to take the initiative and lead them. They appeal to the hearts of the people. People love them and follow their instructions. They sacrifice their lives for their principles. They are true to their word. Whatever they promise, they deliver it.

Visionary leaders give a destination to an organization and don't worry about actions. You have to innovate, take risks, and set a course of action to realize the dream of the leader. Visionary leaders see their vision and let others see it too. Visionary leaders get the commitment of the team with a compelling and powerful vision. The vision encourages more employee engagement, creating productive teams with extraordinary outcomes.

Visions encourage more employee engagement and create productive teams with extraordinary outcomes. People are free to take the initiative and use their full capabilities to achieve organizational goals. Leaders have different styles; some are visionary, others are affiliative, democratic, commanding, or pace-setting. Visionary leaders use several styles to achieve their objectives. Visionary leaders see the world differently; they have the wisdom to energize people to move forward and never give up till the dream turns into reality. Visionary leaders see the big picture and are not concerned about small routine tasks. They emphasize cohesiveness and encourage others to take action in a cohesive manner. Their teams have high capabilities and give outstanding results. They convert followers into leaders and leaders into change agents.

An organization under a visionary leader plays a leading role in the market. Visionary leaders are real and never give a false picture to others. People have high respect for them and accept them with their hearts. They have status in society due to their selflessness and service for others. Leaders with vision inspire people to the moon and beyond. To realize the vision, you have to create discipline in your life, be persistent, and never give up.

Conclusion

Vision is of paramount importance for any leader. Without a vision, a business will not succeed and will perish in long run. Visions must be compelling and powerful to attract people and get their commitment. Leaders give their vision for the future of the organization. It exists in the future in the leader's mind. It is an image of a better future. Visionary leaders shake the country and bring revolution into the lives of the people. They change perception and use people's energy to achieve their goals. They consistently improve the lives of others. They boost the economy of a country with their compelling vision. Visionary leaders share their vision and also inspire people to realize it.

They are sincere, honest, trustworthy, accessible, dedicated, and committed. They create a culture in the organization where everyone is cooperative, dedicated, team-oriented, and motivated. They create teams that cohesively tackle problems and continuously work on their vision. Visionary leaders are flexible, patient, and persistent; they never gives up. They are focussed on their compelling vision and work day and night to realize it. They inspire others with their initiative. They develop, communicate, and implement their vision. They are not afraid of obstacles and challenges to achieve their vision. They overcome all obstacles and move on.

They are highly regarded due to their care for others. Visionary leaders are selfless and have empathy for others. They consider the emotions of others and share their feelings with them. They are emotionally intelligent and monitor their emotions during any challenge. They show self-control and don't lose their temper in an unfavourable situation. They are agile and resilient. They sacrifice their time and resources for the betterment of their followers. They are like servants of the people and are always available and reachable. They have good communication skills and always communicate with their followers concerning any issue. They encourage others to learn more and to take more responsibility. Their inspiring vision produces more leaders. People see a career enhancement working with them.

Bibliography

Adair, J. (1998). *Effective Leadership: How to Develop Leadership Skills.* London: Macmillan.

Boutros-Ghali, B., et al. (1998). *Essays on Leadership.* New York: Carnegie Corporation.

Covey, S. R. (1992). *Principle-Centered Leadership.* New York: Simon & Schuster.

Covey, S. R. (2004). *The 7 Habits of Highly Effective People: Powerful Lessons in Personal Change. Restoring the Character Ethic.* New York: Simon & Schuster.

http://www.sedl.org/change/issues/issues23.html.

http://www.reliableplant.com/Read/29109/leaders-have-vision.

CHAPTER 3

The Art of Communication

COMMUNICATION IS ONE OF THE most important qualities for leaders; they must be skilled in communication to be effective and give outstanding results. Communication means imparting or exchanging information by speaking, writing, or using other media. Leaders communicate their vision to the people clearly and create a culture of communication. Communication is not done to limited people. Communication can be done in different ways. This may be verbal, or it may be done through email or telephone. It can also be done through meetings. It's of paramount importance that everyone in the organization is aware of what is happening and what is coming.

Leaders communicate inside and outside the organization. All stakeholders are informed of the organization's activities. The general public, donors, and students are aware of the organization. It becomes known for its professionalism and expertise, and it gets attention locally, nationally, and globally. It attracts people through communication. If you are producing a product, you use publicity to attract customers. Communication plays an important role in the development of any organization. It may be vertical or horizontal. Leaders create a culture that is based on cooperation and encourages communication. Communication is the building block of any organization. Communication has a purpose in all business organizations. You transmit your message, and another person receives it, analyses it, and responds to it. You have to make sure that your message is understood the same way you meant. Communication has to be clear, authentic, and assertive. Communication is done by the following means:

- emails/telephone/conference calls/chat through internet
- verbally
- meetings
- presentations
- nonverbally

It is a two-way street. You are in communication with specific people who hear you or read your message.

Email

This is very common these days. The best practice for email is that the message should be concise and specific, to the point, and clear. Leaders have to clearly say what they mean, and messages should only be sent to relevant people. Chat through business Skype is also another way of communication. Leaders can chat when it is really needed, but it should be specific and to the point. When you receive an answer for a business-related issue and need more feedback, you should not bother again and again quickly if you expect the same answer. It is a very useful business tool if properly used.

Verbal

Face-to-face communication is useful for sharing information, sharing a business issue, giving instructions for action, making inquiries, and so on. The message has to be very clearly understood by the recipient.

Meetings

This is another important means of communication. If some message has to be communicated or a decision to be taken, a meeting can be held. Good leaders should explain why a meeting is held; it should have a purpose, agenda, specific agenda points, conclusion, and feedback.

An hour meeting with twenty people is equal to twenty hours, i.e., two and half working days of a person. If the meeting does not meet its purpose, you have wasted twenty hours. If the communication can be done without a meeting, there is no need for the meeting.

Presentations

A presentation is another means of communication, sharing information about some important issue.

The outcome of any communication is to inform an individual or an audience. The desired purpose of any communication is understanding. Communication channels include the internet, social media, Facebook, Twitter, YouTube, and so on. They also include radio, TV, letters, brochures, circulars, and directives.

Nonverbal Communication

It is said that verbal communication is only 3 per cent and 97 per cent is nonverbal, including body language. Your body speaks itself. The way you move and the way you talk give information to others. The way you dress and the way you walk communicate your message.

Leaders are good communicators. They communicate a clear message to the audience. Their message has a purpose, and others hear it, understand it, and take action on it. Communication is of paramount importance in the viability of any organization. A culture of communication is created where people continuously communicate with each other. Good leaders convey their message across the organization. Communication is done through different channels (e.g., verbal, email, indirectly through others). Leaders communicate their vision, goals, objectives, and strategy across the organization.

Communication plays an important role in the success of any organization. Good leaders clearly communicate with colleagues their vision, objectives, and goals; there is no ambiguity. Communication is information sharing. Through communication, people are updated about events, strategies, and goals. Communication gives you power; you are more aware of the organization and its people. It ensures that the organization is in line with the strategy and goals. Any shortcomings are overcome on time. Good leaders get information about the concerns and problems of the staff.

Clear communication paves the way for success. The purpose of communication is to inform the audience about a decision, a problem, news, achievement, or action. Good and effective communication leads to success, and lack of communication creates many problems, issues, and ambiguities. When there is an issue, this happens mainly due to poor communication. Inspiring leaders are good communicators and convey their message to all stakeholders with clarity and without ambiguity. Different channels for communication can be used, depending on the need and the message to be conveyed. For example, leaders may want to update all members of the organization about a certain development; they call a meeting and deliver a speech and answer any questions raised; everyone is informed. Conference calls can be held for an important issue concerning people who are working in the remote area. With the development of new technology, many sources of communication are available. People can be connected from one corner of the world to the other. With this modern technology, the world has become a global village.

The ability to communicate depends on the ability to receive. Good leaders are also good listeners. Leaders convey their vision to the people, which gives them a sense of improvement. Leaders must show a sense of service, and it should prevail over their personal agenda. Sometimes, leaders don't listen to others and go ahead with a plan that creates big problems; the people will react to it. Good leaders have to take responsibility. They take advantage of any opportunity while others will take it for granted. They are in constant communication with others and share information them. They don't keep others in dark. Good leaders get consensus of an issue of common concern and find a solution. They are well informed about the problems people face and try their best to find a way out. They are proactive, try to improve the economy, and are concerned about continuous growth.

They occupy the hearts of the people. People become hard workers and change the fate of their nation. People feel that the problem of their nation is their problem. Everyone contributes to the development of the country. As a result, a prosperous society emerges, and the nation becomes a model for others. People live with strong values and feel a sense of responsibility.

Leaders have to convey messages in a respectful way. Their body language has to be in line with their message. At times, people complain that information is limited to the inner circle of the elite, and they are unaware of it. People should not feel excluded. The decision-making process has to be done through consensus, and everyone has to give an opinion. People have to be free to share their views about issues that concern everyone. A decision has to be communicated and shared with everyone.

Leaders by virtue of their moral character, vision, and communication are recognized internationally. National leaders are very transparent and don't keep things of public interest secret; they share information with people on a routine basis. They take people into confidence about issues and inform them how to solve them. They are open to accepting new ideas. Leaders use mass media, newspapers, and magazines to convey to the public government activities for the benefit of the people. People have the opportunity to give their views about issues, problems, and government activities, and they can propose solutions. One communication skill is public speaking, by which you can communicate your message. When you speak to an audience, you have to be confident and careful about how you speak. People judge you by your gestures, your tone, and the words you use. Public speaking is a good tool for communication. When you speak, people read your body language.

Leaders should have a positive attitude and communicate their message clearly; they should make sure the people understand it and give feedback. People don't like negative attitudes. They have to be authentic and mean what they say. Effective communication is at the heart of business success. People see leaders the way they speak to them. You need to maintain good rapport with the people you speak to. Your body language has to be in line with your words. Others have to feel that you have concern for them. You need to show them empathy, which is another key quality of a leader.

Leaders build up long-term relationships with people which are based on trust and friendship. Playing with your mobile while speaking to someone is rude and disregards their feelings. It is important that you pay close attention to whoever you speak to. You need to use clear language and avoid slang. They can give feedback on what they understand. Communicating with a purpose is important.

Another quality of leaders is that they are well aware of who is who and who is doing what. They are in direct communication with managers and keep themselves updated. They chair the meetings and arrange meetings now and then. They are also in contact with outside stakeholders like board members. They present reports about the activities of the organization, its expenses, and its progress to the board members. They evaluate the organization and correct any shortcomings faced by the organization. They also make sure that all activities are in line with the organization's goals and strategy, and there is no diversion. They also make sure that all resources are available for all tasks. They have to be very professional in their job and well informed about the organization. They have to be good speakers and communicate their message to the audience through channels suitable for the message. People have to give them feedback, comment on their activities, and give their opinion. They accept good ideas. They continuously make changes for betterment of the people.

Communication plays an important role in leaders life. They need this skill all the time. This is an art to make your message beautiful before you convey it through any channel. But it is also important how you communicate. In an office environment, leaders will use meetings, phone, Skype, and conference calls to communicate their message to others. If there is an important issue or information they want to communicate to everyone, they will call a meeting and deliver a speech. Leaders are good public speakers. They have to know how to speak.

You have to be careful which words you use. Words give a powerful message and can change the mood of others. If you use nice words, it will affect others a certain way; they will regard you and have respect for you. If you use bad words, you can destroy others. Words are a bond between you and others. With words, you reach agreement and understanding. If people trust you, then they take your wording very seriously.

Words play an important role in the life of a leader. National leaders need to be careful all the time when speaking. They cannot hide anything and have to be prudent. Their words are noticed and shared via mass media. In an organization, there is also nonverbal communication. When you speak, your body language should not contradict you. It is very easy for people nowadays to read body language. Always keep a smiling face so others will smile with you. Keeping eye contact when you listen means you are giving attention to the other person. Looking here and there while speaking shows disregard for the audience.

Good communication skills can make you outstanding. Poor communication skills will damage you. You may have a powerful message, but if you convey it in the wrong way, it will not be heard. Public leaders have to communicate with the public all the time. They have to keep the public informed of the progress of their vision; they need to be good public speakers. Visionary leaders don't make hollow promises. What they say, they deliver.

Communication has to be authentic and reliable. Sharing unauthentic information is not communication. In any communication, ethics should be given high consideration. People judge your words and actions. Actions speak louder than words. Your words should lead to action and implementation. Leaders have to communicate to people what they are doing in the public interest. Leaders are judged by their communication power, promises, delivery, and actions. They have to make it known to followers that they are working day and night, selflessly, for their betterment, and they have no personal interest. Their only interest is the happiness of the people. They consume their energy for their followers.

Communication has a purpose; it's not purposeless. When you need to communicate with someone, any type of communication needs care, and proper words have to be used to convey it. How communication is done is important. You have to consider the audience when you deliver a speech. If you are giving them news about a change, you need to use proper wording to convey it.

Conclusion

Communication is of paramount importance for leaders, and they need to be highly skilled in it. Most of the time, they go to meetings, meet visitors, make presentations, and communicate their vision. Communication is an art; you need to design your message with beautiful words before it goes out. You need an expanded vocabulary so you can use a variety of words. If you write the same way every time, people will find you predictable.

Without good communication, you cannot run a business. You need a proper communication system. Your interaction with other people is significant. Communication should not be boring. People have to be comfortable with it. Great leaders, when speaking to an audience, tell stories to attract their attention and keep their speech interesting. When you give a presentation, keep eye contact with individuals turn by turn so that everyone thinks you are speaking to them. Engage the audience and ask questions; otherwise, they will not listen to you, and their minds will be absent.

Leaders have to be verbally eloquent and expert speakers. They have to meet people of different cultures and know about how they communicate. For example, in Western culture, when you speak to a person, you need to keep eye contact with the listener, which means you are paying attention, and that person has also to keep eye contact with you. In some Asian cultures, if an elder speaks to someone, listeners have to keep their eyes down on the ground. If they keep eye contact with the speaker, it shows disrespect for the elder. Also, women never look into the eyes of a man.

Communication through body language differs from culture to culture. In every culture, you need to use your body movements during speaking, especially when you are addressing a big gathering of thousands of people. You have to use your hands to emphasize your point. Your gestures give meaning to the audience. It is important that you don't make promise you cannot fulfil. You need to do your utmost effort to deliver what you say so people understand you are doing everything.

Leaders with good communication skills say what they mean. They will fulfil their promise, whatever it takes. As leaders, communications have to be real and authentic. People will take an interest in listening to you if they don't think your words will vanish in the air. People will try to reach you for their problems. Communication has to be very clear and show the knowledge and experience of the communicator.

Communication reflects your image, morality, and ethics. Projects often fail due to lack of communication. Problems also arise due to poor communication. The required information is not transferred on time when needed, and as a result, issues arise. Adequate communication across the organization will avoid many problems. Communication has to be done when needed. Communication is the key to your success. Everyone in the organization has to be an expert in communication. Poor communication will damage your purpose.

Bibliography

Adair, J. (1998). *Effective Leadership: How to Develop Leadership Skills*. London: Macmillan.

Boutros-Ghali, B., et al. (1998). *Essays on Leadership*. New York: Carnegie Corporation.

Covey, S. R. (1992). *Principle-Centered Leadership*. New York: Simon & Schuster.

Covey, S. R. (2004). *The 7 Habits of Highly Effective People: Powerful Lessons in Personal Change. Restoring the Character Ethic*. New York: Simon & Schuster.

CHAPTER 4

Delegation and Motivation

DELEGATING AUTHORITY MEANS ALLOCATING POWER to subordinates to achieve more effective results. Power goes downward to subordinates from managers. Delegation is the first rule of an effective leader.

Leaders may be overwhelmed with routine work; they cannot perform every task themselves. They have to delegate others to perform some tasks on their behalf. They have to delegate repetitive nonessential tasks and allocate their time to more important things, like preparing the organization's strategy, meeting investors, and so on. They concentrate on key goals and objectives of the organization. They spend their time meeting with visitors, travelling, giving presentations, and representing the organization outside.

People are trained for specific jobs. The delegated person has the same responsibility as you have. That means that functions and powers are decentralized to the ones who are on the spot. Delegatees have to ask the central authority for help dealing with an unclear situation. They have to take action in the best interest of the organization, government body, or corporation by using the authority they are delegated. Leaders cannot act as leaders and manage at the same time. Management tasks are delegated to subordinates. When delegated, tasks are performed quickly, with no need to ask authorization from the central authority. The delegation of authority can work in ministries, corporations, NGOs, and other institutions. The delegation of authority is very important for the expansion of a business. It plays a key role in organizational development. Delegated authority increases responsibility given to the delegated persons, who have to be very careful using it. Any carelessness will have a high impact on the organization. Delegation may be financial, personnel, administrative, or commercial.

How delegation is done?

First, delegators have to think about whether the person is capable of doing the job in an efficient way. They have to see that the person they delegate is efficient. The responsibility is transferred, and accountability is also transferred. They will be given full independence following rules and regulations to do the job. They will be answerable for any deviation. They have to ensure that their delegating power contributes to organizational objectives.

Before accepting delegation, delegatees have to decide if they are capable of doing the work. If not, they can refuse it. The aim of delegation is to reduce time and run an organization more effectively. At times, delegatees are in a remote area, and delegation makes sense. They cannot contact the central office for authorization for small things all the time. If they are unable to do the task and depend on others to do the work, then delegation makes no sense. Some argue that delegation is only a responsibility; that is not correct. If you have no accountability, the responsibility is not important. By authority, we mean the power and right of a person to use resources efficiently to achieve organizational objectives. There are several stages in the delegation of authority:

Look for a competent person with efficient knowledge who can do the job.

Discuss the job with the person and determine if it's acceptable. If people are reluctant to accept, they may not be right for the task. Find a suitable person with the desired skills and passion to accept delegated authority.

The transfer of authority takes place with an official announcement. The information should be disseminated across the organization.

Delegates will be monitored from time to time to make sure that everything is fine, procedures are being followed, and the desired results are achieved. Two important aspects of the delegation of authority are ethics and transparency. The delegatees should be persons of high integrity, ethically well known, and correctly and efficiently use organizational resources.

Keep in mind that there will be a periodical audit in order to ensure that business is on the right track and delegation has benefitted the organization, facilitated the job, and is in line with organization goals.

Delegation can become an issue if not properly managed. Feedback should be given to ensure compliance with rules and regulations. Delegates have to demonstrate high responsibility and properly document their transactions. This is also a part of decentralization to facilitate the job and achieve long-term goals of the organization.

With delegation, any organization can develop and expand its operations.

Delegation is a key component of multinational companies. Without delegation, operations become slow and time-consuming.

Delegation of authority is an integral part of the leader's role. Delegation leads to staff development, which results in organizational development. Delegatees, being on the spot, are in a better position to respond quickly to any operational need. Some managers are worried about their staff and do not delegate tasks to them. They doubt they can perform and find an alternative to the delegation. They ask staff ideas on issues instead of delegating tasks to them. Delegation, once given, can also be taken back if it fails due to poor performance.

Delegatees will be provided with the resources required to perform the task and given advice from time to time. With effective delegation, businesses expand, and more and more jobs are created. Companies become multinational with increased staff. Delegation of authority needs good governance and a good organizational culture. When leaders give their vision to an organization, they create a strategy to achieve it. In order to implement it, they need to delegate some tasks to subordinates, which is done effectively and properly. Delegatees are motivated by added responsibility, which gives them a feeling of importance. They use their full capacity to do the job, which enhances their morale.

Delegation of authority creates new leaders. Delegation has many advantages, but there are also some disadvantages. If delegatees are not trained and prepared to take new responsibility, the delegation may not succeed. They cannot do a job with imagination and need proper guidance. Managers who do not know how to delegate and transfer responsibility can confuse delegates, and they will not be able to do the job as expected.

Trust between managers and subordinates is crucial. If there is no trust between the two, and delegatees are off site, they may misuse their authority for their personal interests, which will damage the organization's reputation and can also result in serious consequences. If the monitoring system is poor and any deviation is not noted and fixed in time, the delegator may see big surprises. Delegating authority with responsibility to people who cannot handle it will have bad results. They may not meet deadlines.

Authority may be delegated to individuals but also from one institution to another. A business's main office may delegate certain tasks to suboffices. The purpose is to move services close to people and reduce concentration at the main office. Every suboffice takes care of people in its jurisdiction. For example, the authority issuing identity card delegates suboffices to receive applications and issue cards to people in their jurisdictions. People find it easier to go to a local office instead of going to the central office. Legislatures delegate to bureaucracies to make policies; for example, a foreign office makes foreign policy on behalf of parliament.

Delegation of authority has to be the core business objective of an organization. You cannot run your business offshore if you do not delegate responsibility. To expand your business, you must delegate to compete in offshore markets. Your offshore manager knows the situation better and is in a better position to respond to market and customer needs. CEOs of multinational companies have to be competent leaders with high integrity. They have to delegate, monitor, make trips, and see the results themselves. In a small business, delegation may not be feasible, but in large businesses, delegation plays a central role. Delegation of authority will multiply your business units with increased staff.

Delegation of Authority Issues

People who are delegated authority may not be aware of the responsibility; they may take it easy and use their power irresponsibly. It's better if there is a system in place which monitors delegatees and gives them feedback on actions not in line with procedures. Issues can be addressed in time, before it is too late.

Delegation of authority should not be confused with decentralization. Decentralization means to move functions that were performed by the central office to suboffices. They are delegated fully to handle the function. On the other hand, delegation of authority is a transfer of authority but only to a certain level. The main authority stays with the central office.

For example, a CEO delegates her director to incur financial expenses up to a certain level for office operations. Anyone acting at this level will have the same delegation of authority. If delegatees give good results, they will be moved to higher positions. With the delegation of authority, delegatees become bound and are responsible for meeting deadlines.

The delegation of authority may be enhanced, decreased, or taken back, depending on circumstances. The delegation of authority may be permanent, temporary, partial, conditional, or unconditional. Companies expand with the increased number of staff, and delegation of authority is needed to meet the needs of customers.

The delegation may be outward. An assignment for a particular function may be given to an ad-hoc committee not under the direct command of the delegator. The delegation is upward where shareholders give delegation to board members who act on their behalf and make strategic decisions. It can be formal or informal. It is formal when based on rules and regulations, or informal when based on conventions and customs. The delegation may be complete or partial. In a partial delegation, delegatees have to contact the delegator to get advice on certain issues.

Proper policy is devised in line with local customs. Junior staff is developed with additional responsibilities. Delegation reduces congestion and expedites operations. It will fail in countries with bad governance, as the situation on the ground will not meet the conditions required for an effective delegation of authority. Lack of trust will make it difficult for the delegator to delegate key responsibilities to subordinates.

Not everything can be delegated. Formulating new procedures cannot be delegated. Recruiting a high-level manager cannot be delegated to junior staff. There must be transparency, proper communication, reporting, and adequate documentation. Delegation avoids micromanagement. When managers delegate tasks, they are not involved in too many things; they take care of essential tasks and don't do low priority tasks that can be done by others.

Another job of leaders is to work through others. They show their presence through the action of others. If you want to create more leaders, you have to delegate, but you have to know how to delegate and what to delegate. Some tasks may not be delegated. Performance feedback cannot be delegated. Disciplinary action and other sensitive tasks cannot be delegated. Other key tasks which leaders have to do should not be delegated.

Delegation creates an environment of trust and responsibility. With delegation, you get the commitment of the staff; they feel involved and have autonomy and independence. Delegation doesn't go without accountability. Delegation goes downward, and accountability goes upward, which is a by-product of delegating authority. In a broad perspective, people delegate their representatives in parliament to make laws and decisions on their behalf. Governments delegate their ambassadors in foreign countries. Diplomats negotiate on behalf of their governments to resolve any conflict using their delegation of authority. In organizations, the board of directors devises policies and strategies, delegating the CEO to implement them.

Without delegation, individuals lose motivation. Whether a business is private or public, it will not survive without delegation to key players who do the job. It keeps the workload balanced. It takes workload to those who are experts in the game. It relieves the manager from overload. It has to be kept in mind that any delegation of authority should be in the best interest of the organization. While delegating, corporate goals, objectives, and strategies have to be kept in mind; delegation has to be in line with them. As mentioned before, it removes unnecessary barriers, eliminates hierarchical formalities, and shrinks the chain of command. The degree of responsibility is equal to the degree of authority in order to streamline the process. One should not exceed the other, which will create frustration. For delegation to be effective, managers have to know what results they expect. When you delegate, you have to know what results you expect from delegates; it must be clearly explained to them. There should be no ambiguity or misunderstanding. The performance standard is known.

In addition, rules and procedures must be very clear. Clarity is fundamental to delegation. Delegatees must be well equipped with knowledge of the rules and regulations. They also have to know their limitations, what they can and cannot do. Delegatees must be given assurance that help is available whenever needed. Delegation of authority should be considered a step forward and an improvement for the organization. The delegation has to be used in a transparent manner with well-organized documentation.

As long as there is trust and cooperation, honest mistakes can be forgiven. All efforts should be made to avoid mistakes that can badly affect the transaction. Delegation is partial; leaders don't lose their full authority. Delegation of authority has to be explicitly written and understood. Delegation can also be oral, but that is not a formal delegation of authority. Delegation of authority creates a meaningful relationship between manager and subordinate. It leads to continuous vertical communication. It makes subordinates feel important and committed to their job.

Adequate resources have to be allocated to delegatees. Without adequate resources, there is a risk of failure. There must be unity of command; delegatees must know who they report to. Delegation of authority is very difficult and challenging, and only good leaders can make it. Some leaders don't delegate. They feel they are losing control and eventually losing their job. They also feel like they're losing importance. With absolute authority, you keep your importance. They also find it difficult to trust others.

Here are three key principles of delegation of authority:

1) It creates creativity and innovation among subordinates. When subordinates are free to work with responsibility, they are more dedicated and committed to work. They use their imagination and find innovative ways to solve problems instead of running to the boss for little things.

2) It improves organizational efficiency. When individuals are committed, it leads to efficiency and expansion. It also results in a better quality of work. Individuals will use their full capacity and intellect to give better results.

3) It helps to create teams, which avoids conflict between management and staff, resulting in positive relationships. When management is not loaded with routine tasks, they dedicate their time to organizational strategy. Too much concentration of works on subordinates will reduce the quality of their work and may not give the desired results.

Delegatees must understand the reason for delegation. They will also be advised about what results are expected by the organization. There are limitations and other factors which hinder delegation. A new organization will be reluctant to delegate authority due to the inexperience of staff. If there is a crisis, delegation of authority is not recommended. Management will not have time to delegate. They will be busy coping with the crisis. Frequent changes also hinder delegation. The geographical situation is another factor. Leaders fear delegating to subordinates located in remote areas, where managers can't see them. They fear losing control over their operations. Lack of proper monitoring will make delegation difficult.

Some managers consider it time-consuming. They think that explaining a task to others is a waste of time; they'd rather do it themselves. Some managers need to control all other operations and want to do everything themselves. Some managers have a wrong perception of individuals who may have made mistakes. If you do the job, you'll make mistakes. If you don't do anything, you will not make mistakes. Managers have to see reality. Some managers want perfection and don't trust others. They do things themselves to do it the right way.

Someone said, "If you do everything yourself, your business will never grow more than what you can personally handle." With delegation, staff members are more fulfilled, are satisfied, and have little fear of losing their jobs.

But you have to see how far you can go with the delegation of authority. You can motivate your staff to go the extra mile. If you have authority, your staff will comply with your order. If you have good relationships and delegate tasks to them, you can get their commitment. With micromanagement, delegation does not work. Staff feels undermined, undervalued, and controlled. They lose interest. Managers will not be able to devise a strategy without delegation. The business will shrink or fail to grow. Managers think they can only do a good job, and if they don't, others will keep them down. This harms the company, and they cease thinking for themselves. Such thinking and justification sabotages delegation of authority and creates stress in both staff and managers. They have to know the advantages of the delegation of authority and how much they will benefit from it. Delegation of authority has to be planned and done in a structured way.

Conclusion

Delegation of authority is of paramount importance for organizations, government bodies, and political institutions. Without delegating authority, you cannot run a business effectively. Delegation of authority has to be properly managed. Effective leaders can delegate in an efficient manner. Delegation of authority is complex and difficult; only competent and efficient leaders can handle it.

Delegating authority has three elements: responsibility, authority, and accountability. Responsibility has to be balanced with authority. One cannot exceed the other. Leaders cannot do everything themselves; they have to delegate some tasks to subordinates to avoid routine tasks that others can do. This gives them time to focus on other important things like strategy, vision, mission, meeting with board members, and planning changes.

Delegatees have to be properly trained and prepared for increased responsibilities and be aware why they were chosen for the delegation. Delegation of authority creates a meaningful relationship between manager and subordinate. Delegatees are motivated by being given more responsibility. They work with more dedication and commitment. They finds it an opportunity for promotion. Delegation of authority has to be properly monitored and individual performance measured.

Delegation expedites the operation process, and responsibility goes where it is needed. It expands your business and increases productivity. Without delegation, the organization perishes. If leaders do everything themselves, the organization will not grow and they will have little time to devise business strategy. As a result, the business will lack vision and be unable to compete in the volatile market.

Bibliography

Adair, J. (1998). *Effective Leadership: How to Develop Leadership Skills*. London: Macmillan.

Covey, S. R. (1992). *Principle-Centered Leadership*. New York: Simon & Schuster.

https://www.anzam.org/wp-content/uploads/pdf-manager/2158_JOINER_ BAKALIS.PDF. Accessed 3 Aug. 2020.

https://www.academia.edu/22140803/Delegation Authority and Responsibility Removing the RhetoricalObstructions in the Way of an Old Paradigm. Accessed 3 Aug. 2020.

https://hbr.org/2017/10/to-be-a-great-leader-you-have-to-learn-how-to-delegate-well. Accessed 3 Aug. 2020.

http://www.wright.edu/~scott.williams/LeaderLetter/delegating.htm#The%20Very%20Short%20List%20of%20Things%20That%20Shouldn%EF%BF%BDt%20Be.

http://www.iibmindialms.com/library/management-basic-subjects/principle-practice-of-management/delegation-limitations-merits/. Accessed 8 Aug. 2020.

https://journals.sagepub.com/doi/full/10.1177/2053168016632001. Accessed 8 Aug. 2020.

https://www.theguardian.com/careers/careers-blog/delegation-how-to-guide.

https://www.nytimes.com/2008/04/29/business/smallbusiness/29toolkit.html. Accessed 8 Aug. 2020.

https://www.ft.com/content/f29cfff8-df40-11e2-881f-00144feab7de.

https://www.ncbi.nlm.nih.gov/pmc/articles/PMC5461250/.

"Leaders' Behaviors Matter: The Role of Delegation in Promoting Employees' Feedback-Seeking Behavior."

https://gbr.pepperdine.edu/2010/08/the-fine-art-of-delegation/.

https://core.ac.uk/download/pdf/144980434.pdf.

https://www.econstor.eu/bitstream/10419/156751/1/17107-66665-1-PB.pdf. 23 Aug. 2020.

https://www.enclaria.com/2019/02/05/seven-essential-traits-of-a-change-agent/. 23 Aug. 2020.

CHAPTER 5
Self-Awareness and Self Discipline

Self-Awareness

THIS QUALITY IS IMPORTANT IN today's world. It is the ability to observe, examine, and recognize your own thoughts, emotions, and feelings. When Socrates was asked to condense his knowledge and wisdom in one sentence, he replied 'know thyself'.

Most people want to have a happy and controlled life. When we observe, examine, and study ourselves, we compare our behaviour with our internal subconscious values and principles; we become self-conscious of ourselves. This is a continuous process. We have to monitor our stress, thoughts, emotions, and behaviour, and see our reaction to external events under different circumstances. This helps us to improve ourselves.

Self-awareness is of paramount importance; it paves the way for your development, fulfilment, and advancement. We have seen in history that big leaders are self-aware. There are two types of self-awareness: internal and external. You have to see yourself in your own eyes. Think about your view of yourself. Is this perception or reality? Work on yourself, and change your behaviour if necessary. Align your ideals with your current behaviour.

Compare yourself with your standards. How does your behaviour match your standard of correctness? This is the fundamental tool for self-awareness. It helps to stop behaviours that are not compatible with our core values and adopt new behaviours that represent those values better. Self-awareness is a critical tool that helps you reach the highest level of job satisfaction; it helps you be a better leader.

You also have to see yourself through the eyes of others. How do they see you? What is their view of you? Is this a perception or reality? It's advisable to get feedback from your peers, colleagues, and friends. The feedback should be from trusted people. But the problem is, as leaders become more powerful, people are less likely to give them feedback. You can become a better leader by understanding how employees see you. You can improve your relationship with them.

Daniel Goleman (1995) developed the theory of emotional intelligence. It is defined as the ability to manage and control one's emotions and the ability to control the emotions of others. It has five components: self-awareness, self-regulation, motivation, empathy, and social skills.

Emotional intelligence is about knowing your internal states, resources, preferences, and intuition. Self-awareness is a cornerstone to emotional intelligence. It's the ability to monitor your thoughts, feelings, and emotions from moment to moment. The more you understand yourself (in other words, the more you are aware of yourself), the more successful you will be in life. It has been observed that great leaders are aware of their feelings, thoughts, and emotions.

Emotional intelligence goes beyond this; you have to know the feelings of others and be able to influence them. With self-awareness, you can control yourself in times of unforeseen trauma and accident. After observing yourself for some time, you can change yourself. You may improve your behaviour and get rid of unnecessary thoughts or feelings which keep you busy for nothing and keep you from moving forward. With self-awareness, you are more effective, you can know your strengths and weaknesses, and you can work on them. Self-awareness helps managers develop their skills and become more effective and successful.

Motivational speaker Bob Proctor said, "Be yourself."

Anthony K. Tjan writes in *Harvard Business Review,* "There is one quality that trumps the self-awareness which makes the leader more effective." Knowing how other people see them, whether it is perception or reality, is important for leaders to be more effective.

Self-awareness is how you see yourself, your values, attitudes, and feelings, and how other people see you. What is your perception of yourself, and what is other people's perception of you? Is it perception or reality? The more you are aware of yourself, the more you can change your behaviour to be more effective and influential. If you are aware of where your thoughts and emotions are leading you, you can change them. Self-awareness is vital to controlling yourself, creating what you want, and preparing for the future. It provides necessary ingredients for a strong character, to lead with purpose, openness, authenticity.

The journey to self-discovery is unending. The more you move on this path, the more you become aware of yourself; you are able to control and guide yourself in the right direction.

During an accident, you can observe your thoughts, emotions, and reactions. Your emotions, reactions, personality, and behaviour determine where you go in life. When you're self-aware, you can change perception and interpretation of your thoughts. You can work on your goals and objectives correctly and become more influential. You not only change your perception but also change the perception of others. This can give you happiness and satisfaction.

Self-awareness is also important in relationships. You have to look in the mirror and see through eyes of others and adapt to it. By controlling your emotions, behaviour, and thoughts, you can become more resilient. Monitor your reactions in any situation and try to control them.

Self-awareness gives you the power to be more creative, successful, and fulfilled. Continuously observing yourself and working on change is the key to success.

You have a sharp realization of your personality, strengths, weaknesses, thoughts, beliefs, and emotions. You can also understand others. If you develop self-awareness, your own personal thoughts will change. This will change your mental state and increase your emotional intelligence. Tony Robbins says, "Where focus goes, energy flows."

Your focus, energy, emotion, personality, and reaction determine where you will end up in life. Discovering yourself and the process of self-awareness is not simple. It takes time. You have to monitor yourself and write down your thoughts, beliefs, and emotions in different situations.

The root of all your endeavours is you.

Now we see how to become self-aware.

There are different methods to increase your self-awareness. Here are a few:

Look thoroughly at yourself. Write down your strengths and other qualities you have that stand out. Also, list your achievements you are proud of. Look at your youth and see what has remained, what has changed, and why it changed. Also get feedback from people you trust on how they perceive you.

Keep a journal or notebook. Put your thoughts on the paper. Make it a routine every day or night; write down successes and failures. This will help you develop and go forward. Consider yourself as a leader and how people see you. What are your core values?

Write down your priorities and goals, long term and short term. Break down big goals into small goals and handle them.

Practice self-reflection and see yourself as a leader for twenty minutes.

Do mindfulness exercises every day, and make it a habit.

See what is working and what is not working. What obstacles do you have to achieving your goals.

Your trusted colleagues, peers, and mentors could give you honest feedback. They should not hurt you. They should act as an honest mirror.

Also, consider a feedback system like 360 Degrees.

Why do you do what you do? See your empathy for others.

Change the way you are perceived. Be yourself with more skills and your own values.

Evaluate your behaviour and attitude in the mirror of your standards, priorities, and values. What is your big goal? Who do you want to be? Do you want to be a CEO, a leader, a secretary-general? Be honest and assess your competing priorities; what makes you great?

Be curious and make your endeavour to see your insight. We are responsible for who we become. Never give up. Go on seeking and understand yourself.

If some behaviours are not in line with your values, fine, but leave them behind so they don't block you from moving forward. That enables you to design your lifestyle on your own terms. Focus your awareness of yourself. Explore your feelings, and investigate the source of unexpected feelings.

Begin to notice patterns and trends; define your purpose, your values, your motivation, and anything holding you back from the goal you have always wanted.

Expand to areas of your life that have a greater impact on your lifestyle.

We are not even aware of our habits, routines, impulses, and reactions in our life. We don't control them. They control us.

Self-awareness gives you insight into yourself. This introspection makes you self-aware and helps you control yourself. You can align your feelings, behaviour, and emotion with your internal standards. The more you are self-aware, the more you can develop yourself. Great leaders are self-aware; they know their own perceptions and perceptions of others about themselves. Dr Tasha Eurich says to ask what instead of why when seeing your insight. When you are in a bad mood, ask yourself why you are like that. It gives you a negative sense. You do what you can do to change your mood.

Self-Discipline

Discipline is a key component for success. In order to do your job, you have to be self-disciplined. Discipline means you impose some laws on yourself; you follow them in order to achieve your goal. You are in control all the time and are disciplined enough to meet challenges. Why do you have to be self-disciplined? Self-discipline is needed to achieve your aims.

Once you make a commitment, you have to work hard and discipline yourself in order to achieve your objective. You have to change your habits and routines in order to achieve your goals. You need to develop good time management skills and stick to them. Most successful people are self-disciplined. Self-discipline is the bridge between your goal and its achievement. You need discipline for any success. Self-discipline narrows your life and keeps your focus on your goals. With self-discipline, anything is possible. Confidence comes from self-discipline and training.

Here are a few ways to discipline yourself:

Remove distractions. Eliminate temptations; don't listen to your phone, and keep your desk organized. Don't go to social media all the time. Social media kills your time. If you spend your day on social media (Facebook, Twitter, etc.), at the end of the day, you're nowhere.

Eat good food with vitamins and proteins and sugar. A good diet enhances your concentration and focus. Make exercising part of your routine.

Don't wait for the ideal time to change a bad habit. It will never come. You have to work under all circumstances. It is difficult to change your routine, as your subconscious resists. But start it slowly, and try to drop bad habits and replace them with new ones.

Reward yourself and give yourself a break.

Forgive others, forgive yourself, and release negative energy into the universe. That only blocks you.

Start with a little thing and go on.

Decide what you want to do differently and do it.

Businessman and author Harvey Mackay says, "It doesn't matter whether you are pursuing success in business, sports, the arts, or life in general: The bridge between wishing and accomplishing is self-discipline."

The ability to discipline yourself to achieve your goals will guarantee your success.

Achieve success by your own rules, and build a life you are proud to live. Discipline is the key to achieving goals. Habit is a way that leads you to self-discipline.

There are other ways to discipline yourself. Here are a few of them:

We have to be thankful for what we have. Gratitude gives us happiness and satisfaction.

If you worry that others have things you don't, it will create negative thoughts, and you will live a deprived life. Worry and jealousy are the opposite of gratitude. If you are happy with what you have, then you release negative thoughts into the universe.

Always try to forgive others if they hurt you. It will help you sleep well, with no stress. You will always be in self-control.

Pray every day. It will give you satisfaction and happiness.

Set your goals, and actively work on them. When you write down your goals, it will give you momentum and keep you disciplined. Track your progress towards your goals.

Good rest and sleep will give you energy and discipline. Try to sleep at least seven hours a day.

Keep everything in an organized way if that is your office, home, car, or your briefcase. Your items should be easily accessible.

Be a good time manager and avoid distractions from your daily work. Prioritize things. Use the 20/80 rule (Pareto principle): 20 per cent of your effort will give 80 per cent of results.

Always be persistent and never give up. Work daily on your goals.

Practice self-discipline, and don't hurt yourself anymore.

I am writing this book so that others can benefit from it. Benefiting others is much more motivating than doing things just for yourself. It is hard to achieve goals, and it's easy to give up. Achieving goals takes a lot of work at a sustained period before it provides a pleasure. If you don't develop self-discipline, you can face many problems, like health issues, distractions, procrastination, and financial problems.

Victories come from success and failure. Failure means you tried. So it is a victory from the start. It also means you learned something. Failure is a victory, and success is also a victory. No matter what your result is, you can see it as an opportunity to learn. Do it differently if your result is a failure. Get support from others; share your goals and get support.

When you are passionate about your goals, this will keep you motivated and disciplined. Passion and desire give better results than talent.

Leaders with self-discipline have personal control over their thoughts and actions; they can express their emotions in a positive way. They are proactive and well prepared. They don't react to every demand or request. They are well organized and able to persist in the face of difficulties. Through self-discipline, leaders share their confidence with their followers, whom they rely upon for good decisions. As a result, they increase their capacity to influence others.

Bill George (2004) suggests that your values are transformed into actions through self-discipline. Your actions represent your values. With self-discipline, you do what is needed.

As a means of maintaining a balance between professional and personal roles, self-discipline is an important component of effective leadership.

Brian Tracy, an author and motivational speaker, advises that there is no secret to success; there is only one principle to follow which will guarantee your success, and that is self-discipline. This is a habit, a practice, a philosophy, and a way of life. Tracy says to focus on the most important, high-value tasks first and then do low-priority tasks. You should write a list of goals and concentrate on high-value tasks.

Then there is the discipline of planning. Every minute of planning saves you ten minutes of effort. There is 1,000 per cent return.

Discipline is of paramount importance for your success. Without discipline, you go nowhere. If you make a commitment, you need to discipline yourself to abide by that commitment. Great leaders are disciplined and punctual. Anything is possible with a disciplined life. It is now more complicated to discipline your life because of social media, which can distract you all the time. Disciplining yourself is hard work. You have to change your habits, impose some laws on yourself, and respect them. You have to say no to all distractions, temptations, and untimely requests, and strictly follow a disciplined path, which will ultimately give you success. If you say yes to everything, then you are nowhere and just reacting to requests. You are working on the agenda of others. With discipline, you are in control and proactive.

Self-discipline is necessary in all walks of life. With self-discipline, your life will be happy and successful. As a leader, if you have a big vision for the future, you need a strong discipline to realize your vision. Very few people live a disciplined life. It requires sacrifice, strong commitment, and consistency. Once you have a goal, write it down, and fix a time every day to work on it. For example, let's say you want to write a book and decide to write a thousand words per day. You write four thousand words in one day but then don't write anything for ten days. It will be hard for you to finish on time.

If you don't discipline yourself, then you will not be in control of anything. Life will control you. You need to change your habits, which is not easy. Habits are power. Once you adopt a good habit that is in line with your standards and goals, then you will work on your goals easily without even realizing it. You need self-discipline for everything. You can keep your relationships with friends, family, colleagues, and others. You become a good time manager, and everything is possible for you. You can solve problems and cope with complex issues.

Self-discipline narrows your life and keeps you from taking on too many tasks. You only work on achieving the goals on your list. You become yourself and live life on your own terms. You'll get a reputation for discipline, and people will not encroach on your time whenever they want. With self-discipline, you'll be promoted and feel more fulfilled. You'll live a balanced life and have time for your family and friends. You'll have a balance between work and your personal life. You are in control of your life and know when to do what. With self-discipline, as a leader, you can achieve the goals of your organization.

Without discipline, you react to external pressures. You are not in control of your life. Other people or external circumstances control your behaviour. With discipline, you are in control of your own life, and no external force controls you. You manage your time properly and are not distracted by others. Self-discipline has a purpose. Changing habits and routines takes sacrifice. You need to say no to some actions. You don't need to say yes to everything. You need to have proper planning for your life goals.

With self-discipline, everything is possible. With self-discipline, your life becomes more focussed. Your days and weeks are scheduled. People have big goals in life, but if they lack discipline, they don't succeed. Discipline is not easy; it takes sacrifice and self-management; close the door to distractions that encroach on your time. Follow the 20/80 rule (Pareto principle), which means doing 20 per cent of tasks that will give 80 per cent value for your business; 80 per cent of production will come from 20 per cent of inputs.

If you are very ambitious to realize your dreams and vision, you need high discipline. You work on your dreams and goals till the end, without interruption. If you start working on your goals but then stop to do lower priority tasks, this is not self-discipline. You will not succeed in this way. With self-discipline, you have to keep to your promise and work on your goals continuously, without interruption. If your vision is powerful, and you give it high value, you will discipline yourself, whatever it takes. You have to make it. You have to be truthful and honest with yourself; don't cheat yourself.

Self-discipline will make you more effective, improve your reputation, and give you a place in society. You fulfil whatever you promise to yourself. You need powerful goals and compelling visions that attract you like a magnet. It will force you to be disciplined and continuously work on your goals. If you are not disciplined, your vision will perish, and you will never realize it. As a leader, you have an abundance of work that takes your time. Self-discipline is the best solution for your workload. You need to be highly disciplined to cope with challenges. You need to take care of vision, strategy, meeting with different stakeholders, travelling, meeting with media. This takes time management and discipline. Without discipline, you will be wandering around with a purposeless life. At the end of the day, you will have done nothing and will be nowhere. Circumstances and workload will control you. You need to be above everything and proactively take action with self-discipline.

Conclusion

Self-awareness is the key quality of great leaders. The dilemma with many leaders is they are not self-aware. When Socrates was asked to define wisdom, he said, "Know thyself." If you know yourself, your strengths and weaknesses, then you can work on them. You have to see yourself through the eyes of others. How is your image? How emotionally intelligent are you? Always monitor your emotions and reactions in a given situation. If you know it, then you can work on it and improve yourself. For example, after an accident, you can see your reactions and emotions. Get feedback from peers, colleagues, subordinates, and others, and continuously work on yourself. Your self-awareness should not be a perception of yourself but a reality.

As Dr Tasha Eurich, a motivational speaker, says, "If you are more self-aware, you are more effective, promotable and more fulfilled." People rarely give you feedback; it's your responsibility to work on yourself. The more you are self-aware, the more you will be successful.

Then comes self-discipline. Leaders need to be self-disciplined. Self-discipline is the bridge between goals and accomplishment. You have a purpose in life. You have goals and objectives. In order to achieve your goals, you impose some laws on yourself and work on your goals every day. This is the only thing that will lead you to your destination. Without discipline, you will not be able to control yourself. If you don't discipline yourself, you will go nowhere. Time or other people will control you. With self-discipline, you live your life on your terms. It narrows your life and removes distractions and unnecessary things; you only work on your goals. This is the key for any successful leader.

Bibliography

Adair, J. (1998). *Effective Leadership: How to Develop Leadership Skills*. London: Macmillan.

Boutros-Ghali, B., et al. (1998). *Essays on Leadership*. New York: Carnegie Corporation.

Covey, S. R. (1992). *Principle-Centered Leadership*. New York: Simon & Schuster.

Covey, S. R. (2004). *The 7 Habits of Highly Effective People: Powerful Lessons in Personal Change. Restoring the Character Ethic*. New York: Simon & Schuster.

"Energy Flows Where Attention Goes—Focus & Energy." https://www.tonyrobbins.com/career-business/. Accessed 13 Dec. 2020.

Gardner, J. W. (1990). *On Leadership.* New York: The Free Press.

George, B. (2004). *Authentic Leadership: Rediscovering the Secrets to Creating Lasting Value.* (Inglese) Copertina flessibile – 28 lug 2004.

George, B. "Authentic Leadership." https://www.billgeorge.org. Accessed 13 Dec. 2020.

Goleman, D. (1995). *Emotional Intelligence.* New York: Bantam Books.

"How Leaders Become Self-Aware." hbr.org. Accessed 13 Dec. 2020.

"How Self-Discipline Will Make You a Better Leader." https://www.briantracy.com/blog/category/.

Mackay, H. "The Importance of Discipline." https://finance.townhall.com/columnists/harveymackay/2016/03/28/. Accessed 13 Dec. 2020.

https://www.tashaeurich.com/. Accessed 13 Dec. 2020.

CHAPTER 6

Integrity, Ethics, and Values

INTEGRITY IS ONE OF THE most important ingredients of leadership. It is the key to success. Integrity is defined as having honest, moral, and ethical principles and being of good character. Integrity is one of the fundamental values that leaders need to have. Integrity is the basis on which one keeps trust, relationships, and interpersonal interactions. This is very important for leaders. People should trust them first and then follow.

Integrity means whole and undivided. Your heart, actions, and behaviour should be on the same path. You don't show a different personality at different places. You don't have double standards. You are a person of high character. You keep your values and principles, whatever it costs. You don't show favouritism or nepotism. You will lose friends but never bargain on your principles. Your value and character are also evident in your life. Your followers trust you, and you also get the trust of other leaders, even internationally. People trust you and want a business relationship with you. They invest in your organization and make long-term agreements with you. They believe their capital is safe with you.

People with integrity enjoy good relationships with colleagues, customers, and stakeholders, and people in general. Honesty and trust are key components of integrity.

Leaders with integrity attract people, and they trust them. They want to do business with them. They have principles and behave honourably.

In general, integrity is necessary for society to be viable. In a leadership position, integrity is of paramount importance. If you have no other quality but integrity, you will be ahead of others.

Nowadays, integrity is in short supply. People write books on it. They arrange seminars, pass resolutions, and formulate policies on it. But in real life, this quality is lacking. Leaders with high integrity are willing to do what they say and say what they do. They are honest and set an example for others to follow.

Grenville Kleiser said, "You are already of consequence in the world if you are known as a man of strict integrity." Even more so today. Having integrity is the key to leadership and promotion in life. Your word is your bond. Your no is no and yes is yes. This has been a common quality among great people throughout history. The advantage of being known for integrity is that once you have established that reputation, people are happy to deal with you; investors want to put their money with you because you are trustworthy person.

It takes a long time to get a reputation for integrity in leadership, but once you do, it is truly a big achievement. You may not get rewarded quickly, but you will benefit in the long term with true friends, business partners, colleagues, and people who trust you and can be trusted.

Leaders have to understand that their words, actions, promises, and decisions create the organization's values and culture. Leaders are outstanding for three qualities: ability, benevolence, and integrity. Executive leaders are evaluated on character and competence. Leaders with integrity and competence are a precious asset to the organization and are more effective than those who lack these traits. Leaders have to play role model for integrity and have to reinforce employees in the organization. Regardless of their role, leaders are responsible as role models. They have to ensure compliance at every level with ethical behaviour.

Michael Ray Hopkin (2012) suggests that integrity needs consistency of actions, values, principles, expectations, and outcomes. It needs a deep commitment to doing the right thing for the right reason, regardless of the circumstances. People who live with integrity are incorruptible and incapable of breaking the trust of those who have confided in them.

Leaders have to set proper ethical policies, integrate them into organizational culture, communicate them to all at every level, and make it clear that deviation will be unacceptable.

But it is important that you follow the policies you formulate. You can't expect others to follow a policy you don't do yourself.

As a leader, you have to develop trust among staff which grows through interaction with your teams and sustained application of key principles and values. Creating trust and leading with integrity will give others confidence in your work.

Ethical leaders with high integrity have three qualities: universalism, transformationalism, and benevolence. Universalism represents an understanding of people's welfare, which is a macro perspective approach to work. Transformationalism is in line with the concept of transformational leadership as an activity that inspires others in the achievement of visionary goals. Benevolence focuses on the welfare of others through routine actions. As a process, transformation is the link between universalism, as the externally focussed manifestation of leadership character, and internally focussed benevolent intentions.

As an ethical leader, your job is to create a vision and to inspire others to make that vision a reality. To get employees passionate about what they are doing, leaders have to possess great energy in order to create excitement and achieve results.

Leaders have to focus less on the numbers and more on the values of building a team, sharing ideas, and exciting others. Successfully operating as a values-based ethical leader benefits your team, your organization, and yourself.

Some organizations are value-oriented; there are many advantages to this. Being a person of high integrity with ethical behaviour will give you many advantages as a leader:

- It makes you aware of your long-term priorities and the link between the present and desired values.
- You have a better relationship among team members, keeping in view the differences and clarity.
- You create an organizational culture that develops passion and commitment for organization values.
- You make a connection with the people and brand of the organization that is authentic and trusted.

Leaders who emphasize their values present themselves as models and do the right things for a purpose, without sacrificing their key values. Such leaders become successful in carrying out their strategic vision.

Steve Jobs, CEO of Apple Computer, suggested companies use value-based management to find competent and bright people who care about the same things.

Leaders have to display integrity and good morals and high ethical standards. In general, people expect leaders to be fair, cooperative, impartial, and ethical. Their honesty should be beyond reproach. They should treat everyone equally.

Matthew Kelly, founder and CEO of FLOYD Consulting and author of *The Culture Solution* (2019), said, "What used to be universally accepted as good and true, right and just, is now up for considerable debate. This environment of relativism makes it very difficult for values-based leaders."

I don't agree with this narrow approach. Universally accepted values never change. Key values for human behaviour never change with time or place. For example, speaking the truth is always good anywhere. But this is a key quality of all successful leaders. They present themselves as truthful.

Ethical leadership is defined as "the demonstration of normatively appropriate conduct through personal actions and interpersonal relationships, and the promotion of such conduct to followers through two-way communication, reinforcement, and decision-making" (Brown et al. 2005, 120).

This definition emphasizes normative aspects of conduct. I don't agree with this. Ethical leaders have personal principles and sticks to them under any circumstance; even if they are hurt, they never violate their own values and principles.

The rise and fall of a society or organization depend on its leadership.

The future depends on the ability, morality, and competency of ethical leaders. Ethical leaders will shake and change the world. They honestly and sincerely dedicate all resources to achieving an organization's goals. They are resourceful and utilize all their energy for the betterment of people. They have strong values and never changes them, no matter what the circumstances are.

History has always remembered those leaders with great moral and ethical backgrounds. They didn't enjoy a selfish and luxurious life.

Ethical leaders speak to the heart of the people, and they accept them with their heart.

Keeping your values and following your principles is not easy. It will take you out of your comfort zone. You will have to sacrifice your interests and work selflessly for the interests of others, whatever the circumstances are. But it will pay you. You will get respect from others.

The following are the key qualities of an ethical leader:

- justice
- honesty
- respect
- build community
- focus on team building
- value-driven decision-making
- no tolerance for ethical violations

Justice: Ethical leaders are always fair and just. They are impartial and not inclined to favour friends in official business. They believe in equality and don't discriminate anyone on the basis of colour, religion, cultural background, language, or ethnicity. They always act with justice in all matters.

Honesty: This is the key quality of ethical leaders. They honestly run the business or organization, and stakeholders, staff, suppliers, business partners, and people in general trust them. They also transfer it to subordinates and create a culture of trust where people are safe and are inspired by their behaviour, actions, and treatment. Staff work harder and give extraordinary results. There is no risk of cheating and unnecessary waste of time. People are proud of the leader and the organization.

Respect: Ethical leaders respect staff and never insult anyone. They are self-aware, are emotionally intelligent, and feel empathy for others. They deal with everyone with respect and dignity. As a result, others also respect them. They demonstrate this in their communication, both written and verbal. They have self-control, never lose their temper, and deal with everyone with manners.

Build community: Ethical leaders create groups and teams with common values and goals. They coherently work hard to achieve their goals. They take care of everyone in the team. The goals are set in a way that meets everyone's needs. Everyone in the team is heard and considered. Leaders have no personal agenda; they work for common goals.

Value-driven decision-making: Ethical leaders make decisions by considering all aspects and keeping themselves well informed. Their decision is based on the organization's values. A good and value-based decision will give positive results.

No tolerance for ethical violations: Ethical leaders formulate policies for ethical behaviour and values that everyone has to follow. That is communicated to everyone, and everyone knows what is expected of them. Leaders don't tolerate any deviation.

There is zero tolerance for unethical behaviour.

Conclusion

Ethical leaders live and die for ethical principles and values. They keep their values, whatever it takes. Their values express their authenticity. The success of a country, community, or organization depends on its leadership's morality, dedication, commitment, honesty, and empathy. Integrity is one of the most important qualities of a leader. Integrity and sound moral standards are the basis for all relations. Having integrity will keep you far ahead of other people. Integrity is a fundamental and key ingredient for a leadership position. If you have no integrity as a leader, none of your other qualities will matter. You will quickly lose your reputation. People will not trust you. You will not fulfil your promises.

Leaders with integrity are highly regarded and trusted. If you have integrity, you have principles and moral standards. People trust you, and you keep your promises. You commit to your words. What you say, you mean, and what you mean, you say. You deliver what you promise. You are committed to your goals and vision. You have strong values and stick to them. You take the job, goals, and objectives seriously. All stakeholders trust you. You don't waste time or resources. Every minute of official time is precious for you.

Integrity is the main theme of this book. This is a quality which is in short supply. I think all problems, at a microlevel in an organization or macro level in the country, are due to lack of integrity of individuals, which results in bad governance, lack of trust, poor economy, bad reputation, and bad perception.

When such leaders speak, people do not listen. Happiness will go away from the society. Leaders will also transfer their lack of integrity to others, resulting in corruption and bad practices. Having integrity will pay you a lot. People will think that you are selfless. You also transfer your values and principles to your followers, creating an environment of high trust. People work with their conscience, creating a good perception of the country, organization, or community. Official resources are not wasted, and people don't tolerate corruption. It results in good governance, economic growth, and happiness of the people.

Integrity is the basis for an ideal society. It creates transparency, trust, cooperation, and bonds among people. When you have integrity, you do not lie. You will not be unjust to others. You will not make false claims. You will take care of others' rights.

Broadly speaking, the lack of integrity in leaders has created problems across the world. People are not happy with the rights they deserve; they want to snatch the rights of others. They claim other's land and water. They occupy other territories with false claims. This results in self-interest, mistrust, and a miserable society. Selfishness reigns, and people don't love each other. There is too much control, and people's lives are not secure. They live in fear.

On a micro level in an organization, a lack of integrity will result in a lack of development. There will be too much control. Problems will still arise. Leaders of an organization or corporation have to be seen as models of honesty, integrity, and ethics. Their integrity will motivate others to follow. This will create a culture of values, and the general public will trust it. It will result in high dedication and commitment of the people. This will result in growth and organizational development. The goals of the teams will be achieved. Promises will be met. Agreements with other entities will be respected. The organization will have a better position in society. It will have a good perception and attract others.

Integrity cannot be underestimated. It should not exist only on paper. People have to demonstrate it in their actions and behaviour. Public leaders with integrity must be transparent and disclose their finances to the public. They don't receive gifts for doing their official duty. They don't use official assets for their personal business.

On the other hand, if leaders are not trustworthy, people will be reluctant to do business with them. They give a bad image of their organization or country. An Eastern poet said, "Nations stayed and remained on basis of their morality. When they're morally gone, they were gone."

Good character and integrity have a significant effect on people, which spreads with high speed. People are highly influenced by leaders with high integrity and love them with their hearts. To get integrity, you need to sacrifice and make a sustained effort over a long period of time. You have to stick to your principles, whatever the circumstances are. You have to sacrifice your interests. You need to serve the people, irrespective of their relationship with you. You have to become known to people. People with high integrity don't want a reputation. Their character and integrity get it. A leader of high integrity will also teach others to get a life of high integrity. There is no substitute for integrity. You live a peaceful and satisfying life. You are sincere and don't have stress. You become models for others, and others follow you.

Bibliography

Adair, J. (1998). *Effective Leadership: How to Develop Leadership Skills*. London: Macmillan.

Boutros-Ghali, B., et al. *Essays on Leadership*. New York: Carnegie Corporation.

Covey, S. R. *Principle-Centered Leadership*. New York: Simon & Schuster.

Covey, S. R. *The 7 Habits of Highly Effective People: Powerful Lessons in Personal Change. Restoring the Character Ethic*. New York: Simon & Schuster.

http://www.valuesbasedleadershipjournal.com/issues/vol1issue1/dean.php.

https://leadonpurposeblog.com/2012/01/21/leadership-and-integrity/. Accessed 4 Nov. 2018.

https://www.washingtonpost.com/blogs/guest-insights/post/leadership-character-the-role-of-integrity/2011/04/04/gIQArZL03H_blog.html?noredirect=on&utm_term=.3db9160eb7d8.

https://www.leader-values.com/article.php?aid=576. Accessed 4 Nov. 2018.

https://www.campuspride.org/resources/6-core-values-of-leadership/. Accessed 4 Nov. 2018.

https://www.sciencedirect.com/science/article/pii/S104898430600110X. Accessed 4 Nov. 2018.

https://www.indeed.com/career-advice/career-development/ethical-leadership. Accessed 5 Apr. 2020.

https://yscouts.com/10-ethical-leadership-characteristics/. Accessed 5 Apr. 2020.

https://managementstudyguide.com/leadership-ethics.htm. Accessed 4 Apr. 2020.

https://www.businessnewsdaily.com/5537-how-to-be-ethical-leader.html. Accessed 4 Apr. 2020.

https://www.selfgrowth.com/articles/Integrity_in_Leadership_. Accessed 4 Apr. 2020.

https://leadonpurposeblog.com/2012/01/21/leadership-and-integrity. Accessed 14 Dec. 2020

https://scholar.valpo.edu/ cgi/viewcontent.cgi article=1008&context=jvbl. Accessed 14 Dec. 2020.

CHAPTER 7

Leaders and Change Agents

THIS IS THE KEY CHARACTERISTIC of leaders how they manage change. They challenge the status quo in line with their vision. In today's world, there is a continuous change in business markets with the development of technology, the Internet, and social media, which bring people together. The old-fashioned system has to be evolved and, if necessary, replaced. A change agent has not only to improve operations or reengineer the process but to change the culture of the organization.

Change is necessary to keep it viable in a competitive changing environment. Changing processes and projects is the purpose of many organizations.

The job of a change agent is not easy, as change itself is a complex task. Change agents must study how people work, how they behave, and how they respond to requests and demands. Change agents have to transform their organization to enable it to respond to demands, challenges, and emergencies. Change agents will equip key players with skills and develop contingency plans to respond to unexpected challenges. Change agents are dynamic leaders and well informed about market conditions.

Change agents have to work carefully to cope with the following:

- obstacles from some players
- lack of commitment
- lack of resources
- lack of support

Different change projects need different types of change agents with specific characteristics.

There are different levels of change:

- First, it is seen that there is a need for change in view of different factors.
- Change is clearly mentioned and defined, considering all causes, reasons, and the areas affected, and a formal change process starts.
- The change leader takes initiative and leads the change in uncertain, difficult, and complex circumstances.
- The change leader not only leads the change but also monitors and manages it to ensure that it is moving forward in the right direction and there is no deviation or loss of direction.

In complex projects, change agents need the strong support of recipients in order to make sure they are happy with the change and familiar with the new process. Without the support of all stakeholders, the change will not be successful and will become a hard path for the change agent. Effective change agents will meet all stakeholders and brief them about the change, its different stages, and the resources required for the whole process till its completion. Dynamic change agents share their vision of the whole change stages, difficulties, barriers, and timeframe. They set clearly defined goals that are realistic, achievable, and time-bound. They work on team building and assign specific tasks to specific team members. They delegate to team leaders certain functions they are responsible and accountable for. Change agents need tolerance and patience in an uncertain environment to handle ambiguity, obstacles, challenges, and organizational politics. Change agents have to be good communicators with strong interpersonal skills to influence others and motivate them on the path to change.

They should have strong negotiating skills to convince the stakeholders what is in their best interests. Their job is to challenge the existing assumptions, question the status quo, and replace it with a more effective process, a system that not only benefits the staff and stakeholders but also customers and key partners now and in the future. They have passion, conviction, and confidence; they inspire others and get their commitment to work hard for a better future. They establish a sense of urgency, resist the naysayers, get rid of the pain of change, concentrate their resources, and move forward with a strong commitment. They need a strong strategy to plan the change and complete it. As one leadership consultant said, "Without a strategy, change is merely substitution, not evolution." Change management is no longer only about operational improvement, cost-efficiencies, and process reengineering; it covers the whole culture of the organization, which must be radically changed to be in line with organization goals.

Change is a pain, and people are reluctant to accept it. The change agent's job is to interact with them and convince them that change is necessary and is for their benefit, and also to let them know the cost of not changing. People become familiar with the status quo after several years; changing those behaviours can be annoying.

Change agents are normally experienced workers taken from line management; they are charismatic and have a strong relationship with all stakeholders. They coach people and act as facilitators. They have analytical skills and solve problems. They are a liaison between staff and management.

Change agents take you to a solution. They have strong interpersonal skills, influence people, and get their commitment.

There are a variety of projects that need a change agent. Change agents have to clearly define what change has to be made and determine if it's a process reengineering or operational change.

Change has to be clearly understood by everyone. All key players must be involved and their opinion be considered. Change agents have to understand who is who in the organizational hierarchy and then systematically arrange meetings with people. They have to overcome organizational politics in a diplomatic way. Change agents often meet with people who are not experts in their job, so they must be careful with each step they take.

Leaders as change agents create a network of committed people. They have to work on team building. They have to coach and train team members. They have to lead the change and manage it till the end.

The following are key qualities of a good change agent:

- They are flexible, they listen to everyone, and they value everyone's opinion.
- They are bold and are not reluctant to meet different stakeholders.
- They emphasize team building and create a community of loyal and committed people.
- They take steps which are goal-oriented.

Change agents see all issues very thoroughly. Leaders as change agents are very competent and get promoted quickly. They initiate change and lead it till its completion. They are knowledgeable and have strong communication skills. They have to work in a specific timeframe to meet the deadline and target. They have to continually monitor the progress.

Change agents introduce change and define it, manage it, and lead it through uncertain circumstances. The change could be about a process, operations, reorganization, or a new management structure, or it could be a big change like a merger, acquisition, or outsourcing. Change of any type needs competency, knowledge, commitment, and a lot of work. Change agents are champions of the change; they have big responsibilities.

Managers and executives are expected to be change agents. They must

- know various facets of project organization and individuals
- formulate how the change will happen
- offer guidance and support
- deliver expected results
- persuade others
- initiate implementation

Change agents develop followers and transform them into leaders and develop leaders into change agents. There is continuous coordination between change agents and senior management about the progress of change. They give continuous feedback to management on the progress, issues, and steps necessary to go on. Change agents have to keep track of the progress of ongoing projects. Change is hectic, and they have to overcome all problems and misunderstandings. At times, staff may believe that change will adversely affect their job; change agents have to think from all angles and address many issues.

The role of a change agent has evolved over time. Leaders who led their teams in the time of change were regarded as outstanding performers. When change is needed, change agents have to delegate and galvanize their teams to take action.

"There is nothing more difficult to take in hand, more perilous to conduct or more uncertain in its success than to take the lead in the introduction of new order of things" (Machiavelli 1532, chapter ii). Changes are undertaken to be competitive in the market. Implementing change is a difficult task, and there is a risk of failure.

The reason for failure is at times process, operations complexity, organization structure, and so on. The focus on human resources is ignored. People are the key players in any change. Therefore, change agents must focus on people, their behaviour, attitudes, and their way of work. They must be motivated and inspired to commit to change.

The success of a change depends on the relationship between the change agent and decision-makers. Managers and employees can be trained to make small changes. For big changes, external consultants are hired. They see the organization with fresh eyes and challenge the status quo. But they lack knowledge of internal culture, rules, and regulations.

I think there should be a combination of the two: external change champions and internal change agents.

There needs to be more research done on this important topic. There are several types of agents (Burke 2011; Eikenberry 2011; Mansfield 2011; Thota 2012):

1. Outside pressure: These change agents or pressure groups are outside the organization and use political pressure to make the company change through demonstrations, strikes, and civil disobedience. They seek radical changes.

2. People change technology: The emphasis is on individuals. The focus is on their behaviour and attitude and morale. Individuals are motivated to give the desired results. An internal manager can take the position of change agent.

3. Analysis for the top: This change is related to organizational structure. Change agents study the policies, procedures, and system of an organization and make radical changes to enhance efficiency. New technology is often used to improve efficiency.

4. Organizational development: This is related to the internal process, procedure, culture, interrelation, and decision-making. An internal manager can play this role.

The role of a change agent is to consult, train people, and perform research.

Managers as change agents are beneficial due to their position. Change agents face a lot of resistance from many people. They need to overcome resistance and educate people about these new ideas and their benefits.

Change agents need to make alliances of like individuals to perform different tasks required.

Change may be in a private company or public organization, is a complex job and needs a lot of hard work, efficiency, knowledge, patience, perseverance, and diplomacy. Change in a private company is easier, as there is much freedom with little bureaucracy, compare with a public organization with more complexity.

The only thing which is constant in life is change. In order to be competitive in the market, organizations have to adapt to the changing environment surrounding them. Technology is changing. With the Internet, technology is rapidly changing and improving.

Processes are changing. Not everyone is comfortable with change. You have to change your habits, routines, and behaviour. To start a new life, you need training; you must learn to cope with a changing environment. Back in the 1990s, change meant process reengineering, but the concept of change has changed. It is not only related to processes; it is related to the organization's entire culture. People have to change their behaviour to be in line with the environment or ahead of others.

The conventional way of working in corporations doesn't work. We work in a very volatile world, where nothing remains static, due to great competition and many players in the market. Great leaders understand the environmental requirements and dedicate their energy to make reforms and bring about changes to their organizations. They create a learning environment and change people's behaviour. Under change agents, people become more flexible and adopt a progressive mindset.

Change agents bring change in line with the leader's vision. Change agents will give you a road map to realize the leader's dream for the organization. After all, the vision given by the leader is the ultimate goal and objective. The new process is not for the sake of change but to improve the organization. So the change agent has to handle ambiguity, surprises, and people's lack of interest. They have to hold meetings with all stakeholders and inform them what is change about and how the organization will look after the change. They have to inform everyone that this is needed and will help them achieve the organization's goals. Without change, the organization will be left behind and will not be able to compete with other players.

Change agents have to be highly qualified with interpersonal skills and be well aware of the change they are bringing about. Change agents should have experience; it's better if they have done the job before. What were the results of the change they did before? How successful was it? They should present a model that reflects the organization's environment after the change.

Organizations have to go through many changes. The organization may be at risk, and agents have to see if merging with another company is necessary for its survival. They may bring new technology to the organization to handle day-to-day work more efficiently. They may outsource some services where they can be provided better and less expensively. They may decentralize operations to suboffices who are closer to service receivers. The latest trend in many organizations is to recruit leaders who are change agents.

Change agents have to know the current culture of the organization, its systems, and its defects. They have to know rules, regulations, procedures, organizational strategy, and its mission. They have to know the politics of the organization and its position in the market. Change agents are not so specialized that only certain consultants can handle it. The leader's job has evolved with time and shifting environment. Leaders today have to be highly competent, responsive, and proactive to external demands. Leaders have to be innovative and act as change agents.

With globalization, the world has become interconnected. Leaders should have diversified knowledge. They have to improve the status quo if it doesn't meet evolving external demands. They need a lot of energy to make changes. Change agents have responsibility and accountability. They have to build teams to help them in the change process.

Change agents are accountable for the team's performance. Change agents are effective when they have a good relationship with management and other decision-makers. Their proposals should be considered for acceptance. Change agents focus on results that are in line with organizational goals. They must keep the best interests of the company in mind.

Change not only needs the dedication of people but also a lot of resources. Before going for any change initiative, companies have to consider their budget constraints and resources. Planning is of paramount importance for any change. As a change is implemented, you may see that the allocated resources are not sufficient. Allowing flexibility during planning will avoid such surprises.

Change is unavoidable in today's competitive world. The Internet has brought people closer together. Accessing any information is not a problem. Culture also plays an important role in organizational change efforts. Change agents have to know the audience of change. They have to know how they behave, how they process information, and how they react to change. Culture is the most important factor, and change agents have to study it properly.

As I mentioned before, change agents can be internal, external, or a combination of both. External change agents come with a fresh view of the organization from an outside perspective, but they don't know the culture of the organization. A combination of both is better. People work in a certain way in the organization. Change is not related to a processing or system change; it may also be related to behaviour change. Change is either planned or unplanned. It is a reaction to the external environment or a preplanned change that is enacted systematically.

There are many types of changes. It may be a big change, like a merger, acquisition, outsourcing, downsizing, streamlining the process, or restructuring. It may be a small change, like opening a branch or shutting a department or some other reorganization. Big changes are complex and need a team of experts led by a change agent. Change agents play a leading role. Change is seen as a disruption, an unknown thing. People are naturally reluctant. Changing their mindset is the most difficult part of all changes. People have well-established habits, and altering their behaviour takes patience and time. It is not an overnight job.

To be effective leaders and change agents, people have to have integrity and high ethical standards. This will contribute to their success. Change is also related to the norms of an organization. Operational procedures, rules, and regulations can be changed. Individuals will need several training sessions and a lot of learning to adapt to change. Learning plays an important role in the change process. Learning can help change people's behaviour. Learning is very important to overcoming resistance to change. Leaders and change agents have to be creative and innovative. Change agents have to have passion and strong principles. Nothing should change them. They have to make a difference. They have to see results. According to Bekhard (1969, 101) change agents are "those people inside or outside the organization who provide technical specialist or consulting assistance in the management of a change effort."

The change may not be a financial necessity; other factors may require an organization to change. Change is not limited to a one-time event. It can be a continuous process for improvement. Necessity makes change unavoidable. Some leaders are more proactive than others. In order to be a leader in the market, you have to go through continuous changes. The main aim of the change is improvement and achieving corporate goals. Leaders have to cope with uncertainty and discomfort. They have to mobilize efforts to make change happen.

Effective change agents must have many qualities:

1. Resilience. They have to endure setbacks, resistance, and criticism, but they have to cope with them without giving up. They must have courage and speak out. They have to say the truth, even if people don't like it (especially when the authorities don't like it). They have to honestly give their opinion and plan for changes that are in the best interest of the organization.

2. Empathy. Change agents have to be empathetic and have emotional intelligence skills. They have to see themselves in the shoes of clients to know how they feel about the change. Many clients facing a change feel frustrated; this is justified. Change agents need to build a relationship with clients and take them in confidence.

3. Forward-thinking and courage: Change agents have to think about the future of the organization. They have to keep in mind the future picture of the organization after the change. They should be fully focussed and concentrated on future results. They also have to transfer this to others. They must have the courage to bring change.

They have to communicate their vision about the change frankly and boldly, without any fear. They have to convince themselves that they are selfless and work for the benefit of others. They have to be service providers. They have to have proximity to clients; the closer you are to each other, the easier the change will be.

4. Effective listening: Another quality change agents need is listening. They have to listen to clients, leaders, and managers, and reflect on their ideas. If they hear good ideas, they can take them into consideration. People will try to come back to the status quo, as it's difficult to change a habit. People come back to old habits after some time. You have to keep them in the right direction and make sure they don't return to the status quo.

You need to take action deliberately and with caution. Use powerful words to break old patterns. Leaders and change agents have to think strategically about their goals. The strategy must be in line with the objectives of the organization. They have to use their influence to make the change. Change must first be designed and then implemented. The implementation part is more difficult. It often doesn't go smoothly. You need to do a lot of effort to prepare and make it. You have to speak to people's hearts and heads to get their commitment. Your good relations will make a difference.

Before going through change, leaders have to give a compelling story and reason for the change. For example, "Our leadership position has been damaged by competition and customer service. In order to regain our position, we have to change," or "We are underperforming against industry standards. If we have to survive, we have to change. The change will not only ensure our survival but give us a leading position in the industry."

The change has to be done in a structured way. Change agents have to have the quality of openness. They have to be flexible and open to hearing any comments. They have to be optimistic that change will bring its fruits. They have to apply the model, framework, and tools in a nice way which is attractive to clients. They are very practical and do what they say. They deliver what they promise. They do things in a strategic context. They believe in teamwork and emphasize synergy, which means that whole is greater than the sum of its parts. Change agents need a lot of energy, both physical and psychological. They have to work for long hours to meet deadlines. They need to present the model to clients, leaders, and managers. They need to take the time of the people. They have to make time to meet you. They also have to continue their routine operations. The success and easiness of the change will depend to a large extent on the degree of their closeness to clients. The closer you are to them, the easier it will be to exchange ideas.

Not all change initiatives are successful. They fail due to several reasons:

1. Lack of resources. Change agents cannot work with inadequate resources, financial and human. They are radically changing the system and need sufficient resources to make it happen.

2. Change agents do not have the right skills to make it happen. Change agents are experts; not every leader can do this job.

3. Poor planning. You need structure and planning to make changes. Planning should be done for the whole process till the outcome.

4. Lack of support from management. If leaders do not support it, then change agents cannot go alone and move forward. They need strong support and collaboration from leadership and all other stakeholders. At times, the leader's focus is on the system rather than people. People make a change. The system is run by people.

Conclusion

It is of paramount importance for leaders to be change agents. The job of a change agent is to change the system, culture, behaviour, and mindset of people so they can face new challenges.

In today's volatile environment, the only thing which is constant is change; you can never avoid it. You have to embrace it. If you don't change your organization with a changing world, you will lose your viability. You cannot work with old technology in the modern world. With technological development, technological systems are replaced every five years. Change is not only about operational improvement or process reengineering; it is about radically changing organizational culture. The job of leaders as change agents is very complex. They have to study the organization's culture, procedures, guidelines, strategy, corporate objectives, goals, and mission statement. They need good relationships with internal players who run the business. They need to maintain good relationships with them to get their commitment. They have to listen to everyone to see how the current system is.

At times, outside change agents are hired and work with an internal change agent. Change agents should have the authority to bring any change. This job needs patience, perseverance, and tolerance. Change agents will face many obstacles, as people are reluctant to change. They have to convince them that it is for their betterment. They will have a better life after this change.

Change agents have to overcome resistance. They have to handle those who are against the change and modify their mindset. They are transformers and change the lives of people with new ideas and values.

Bibliography

Adair, J. (1998). *Effective Leadership: How to Develop Leadership Skills.* London: Macmillan.

Boutros-Ghali, B., et al. (1998). *Essays on Leadership.* New York: Carnegie Corporation.

Covey, S. R. (1992). *Principle-Centered Leadership.* New York: Simon & Schuster.

Covey, S. R. (2004). *The 7 Habits of Highly Effective People: Powerful Lessons in Personal Change. Restoring the Character Ethic.* New York: Simon & Schuster.

https://www.econstor.eu/bitstream/10419/156751/1/17107-66665-1-PB.pdf. Accessed 23 Aug. 2020.

https://www.enclaria.com/2019/02/05/seven-essential-traits-of-a-change-agent/. Accessed 23 Aug. 2020.

https://searchcio.techtarget.com/definition/change-agent.

http://www.nationalforum.com/Electronic%20Journal%20Volumes/Lunenburg,%20Fred%20C.%20Managing%20Change%20The%20Role%20of%20Change%20Agent%20IJMBA,%20V13%20N1%202010.pdf. Accessed 19 Apr. 2020.

https://naaee.org/sites/default/files/lunenburg_fred_c._managing_change_the_role_of_change_agent_ijmba_v13_n1_2010.pdf. Accessed 12 Dec. 2020.

https://www.brainyquote.com/ niccolo_machiavelli_131418. Accessed 14 Dec. 2020.

CHAPTER 8

Training and Continuous Learning

ANOTHER IMPORTANT QUALITY FOR LEADERS is to continuously learn new skills. Leaders have to be a readers. With the changing world, you have to be a continuous learner in order to keep up to date on new business trends. Leaders must anticipate what is coming and be able to adapt to it. If you don't learn new skills, you will stay in a static situation and will not be able to keep up with the environment.

How to Learn New Skills

Before reading, ask yourself why, what, and how. Before we go into the details of this chapter, let us see how to learn new skills. People learn in different ways. Reading is the key to learning. Quality learning is important. People say you should learn a thing well enough to teach it. That means input is equal to output.

Learning for the sake of learning is not a goal. What you learn, you have to implement and coach others. Brian Tracy says, "Reading a book on your subject should be your habit." Reading should not be for pleasure. You have to make sure that you retain what you read.

When you read a book, first see what you know about the subject and then ask what you want to learn.

Preread by skimming the book and looking at the contents. Then read, reflect on it, and implement it. Input should be equal to output. Another method is learning for teaching. So capture it and then ask yourself, "How do I use it? Why must I use it?" Motivate yourself.

Information, inspiration, and implementation. Teach what you learn. Explain what you learn. Don't memorize; take notes, turn it into a picture. One thing that's common among all big leaders is that they continue to learn throughout their lives.

Focus more on output than on input. Emphasize quality of input in order to have the quality of output. So learn, reflect, implement, and share.

You have also to know how to learn through different channels. Continuous learning is of paramount importance for leaders. Without learning, you cannot develop yourself and your staff. Your current position is the result of your learning and knowledge. Leaders have to keep learning on their schedule.

Experience also teaches you. You learn from new challenges and the way you cope with them. Organizations become learning companies where leaders encourage everyone to learn new skills to cope with tasks. If you learn more, it will contribute to your personal development. When you learn new skills, you don't remain the same; it changes your behaviour. As a result, you develop yourself, which can develop your organization and also expand the business. You continuously adapt yourself to a changing environment by learning new skills. You succeed in any situation where others fail.

You become a model for your followers.

Continuous Training

You can take a training course to learn more. Many organizations spend a lot on learning. Leaders and managers take courses for executive MBAs that increase their managerial, leadership, and business skills. It is said that knowledge is power. If you have knowledge, skills, and experience, that means you have power. Leaders have to learn how to cope with every new situation.

Organizational Development

Learning contributes to organizational development. When people grow in an organization, the organization also grows. It doesn't stay static. In order to achieve your objectives and goals, you need to always learn. You should always read books on your subject. You have a vision that exists in the future. You have to prepare yourself and your followers to learn new skills to realize your dream. Every day, you have new ideas that come from your learning. You have to read journals and newspapers, and keep yourself informed about the environment, the market, and new business regulations. You need to know about outsourcing, offshore business, decentralization, acquisitions, and mergers.

Leaders have to be dynamic when it comes to learning. The future of the organization depends on the leader's capabilities. There is no better teacher than experience. Experience teaches you how to cope with complex issues. A learned person is confident in any situation and has no fear.

By learning new skills, you find innovative solutions to problems. You get a position due to your knowledge and experience, as a result of your learning. When you go to school, you read some books and are examined on that information. You get a degree that certifies your knowledge and makes you acceptable for a position. Leaders can learn from speeches, videos, conferences, and journals; they need to be informed of the political environment and changes in laws.

Leaders can take courses at the expense of the organization. Learning is a key ingredient for every company. Companies keep a specific budget for staff training and development. With learning, one can be promoted easily and be more fulfilled. In order to achieve your goals, you have to discipline yourself to learn the skills you need. You take certain steps every day to reach your goals. Learning will move you up. Leaders who don't learn are left behind. Leaders create a culture of learning where everyone has a desire for learning.

Technology is rapidly changing. Every five years, you need to change your processes and systems to be in line with new technological developments and inventions. In order to use new technology, you need to train people. As someone said, "What I have learned in life is to learn more." There is no end to learning; it is lifelong.

Learning has to be the foundation of your objectives. Your vision for the organization or company has to include this key element of learning in order to move forward. In a competitive world, you can remain outstanding if you have a habit of continuous learning. Learning makes you more effective, flexible, influential, and promotable. Learning can give you self-awareness, which is of paramount importance for successful leaders. You also have to learn about your competitors, their strengths, and their weaknesses. You have to learn your personal strengths and weaknesses. You have to utilize your strengths more effectively and continuously try to improve yourself. You need to improve your company's perception in the marketplace. Make people under you aware that learning new skills is something they should do whenever they can; they should take courses and learn new skills.

Great leaders are also great learners. They study biographies of other leaders who have left a legacy and are remembered for their achievements. This is common in all great leaders; they learn from every event and situation. Learning helps you both professionally and personally. With learning, you find new ways to solve problems. Business techniques, technologies, and processes are evolving. People throughout an organization should plan for their learning and development, irrespective of their position.

Learning requires passion and aspiration. Your goal will attract you and oblige you to learn new skills. It will help you develop your productivity. You can increase your productivity by learning new skills and enhancing your knowledge. Learning gives you confidence and assertiveness. Leaders with no desire to learn new skills are not fit to lead teams. They will not encourage their teams to learn. Leaders have to keep an eye on the environment, see how their competitors run their business, and determine their approach to learning. The job of a leader is to devise a strategy for continuous learning and training.

Learning needs patience and a consistent effort, which is key for success and development. Learning expands your knowledge. When you learn new things, it changes your thinking, and you see situations from a different angle. It will give you confidence and satisfaction. It will give you the power to handle any challenge. You won't be reluctant to speak at a public event if you are already prepared. You'll be prepared for any uncertainty. Consistent learning should be part of your life. You have to motivate yourself to learn more and more. You must have a vision, and in order to reach your target destination, you need to work hard and take steps every day.

Learning gives you power and lets you change your behaviour and adjust your approach to problems. You can learn in many ways like day-to-day experience, challenges, setbacks, failures, and so on. Leaders learn more from failure than from success. They find success in failure also. They learn new lessons and change their approach. They find a new way to cope with challenges and day-to-day tasks.

Knowledge Management

Knowledge management is one of the key elements leaders must learn. Knowledge management is capturing, sharing, and distributing information. Leaders are concerned with knowledge management of the organization and create an environment where knowledge is easily accessible. They take care of this key asset, which is the organization's strength, and make sure it's easily available. Newcomers are trained and equipped with the skills required for the job. Lower turnover means higher productivity, and the business is not disrupted by the departure of skilled staff. Knowledge management is done in a structured way. It is transferred from one worker to another.

People share knowledge with one another in the office, during breaks, and when meeting in the corridor. Leaders are more effective when they manage knowledge and keep it viable. Learning is also important for political leaders.

They can learn from experience and interact with people; they should also encourage learning for their team. Learning is the key to good governance.

Learning expands your horizon. Leaders should read about successful leaders and study what they did. There is a blueprint that you can see and follow. In order to become a great leader, you have to leave your comfort zone and work hard to improve your skills. You need to learn from your mistakes. Every leader makes mistakes, and you have to accept them. Successful leaders do not blame their mistakes on others. Every challenge gives you a lesson, and you can learn from it. You need to capitalize on your strengths and the strengths of others.

It is also necessary to learn interpersonal skills. You may be working in a multicultural environment with people from different backgrounds. You have to be aware of their culture. Leaders have to understand that they are watched all the time. What you say is multiplied. You have to be careful. Your positive or negative feedback will be multiplied. Leaders have to learn the key skills required for leadership, like public speaking, chairing meetings, and making presentations in seminars. Learning also promotes change and removes your reluctance to adapt to new situations. It multiplies your productivity with modern skills. It leads you to the right decision on time. You should adopt a habit of continuous learning.

When you believe in yourself with confidence and think that anything is possible, it takes you out of your limited thinking. With learning and visualization, you can reach your impossible goals. You have to be persistent in learning and studying any material in your sector. There is tough competition in the twenty-first century; you should be alert for learning and adapting to new situations. You should watch the environment carefully and take every step necessary for your success, whether it is in acquisitions, mergers, outsourcing, decentralization, or process reengineering.

Many organizations and corporations have disappeared due to poor management and ineffective leadership. It wasn't due to resources but lack of knowledge by the leader. When you reach a leadership position, it doesn't stop there. The journey is just beginning; you have to go on and demonstrate your leadership skills. You also have to coach your subordinates, peers, and friends. You should act as a mentor. In manager-subordinate coaching, the influence of authority creates a dynamic relationship.

Leaders are either fostering learning or hindering it. Great leaders create conditions, space, and time for learning. This is part of the corporate strategy, and the budget should be allocated for it. Learning is not only done through training but also through coaching, mentoring, and teaching. Leaders coach staff reporting to them, but having authority can hinder teaching. Subordinates may be reluctant to learn from their superior.

Leaders also mentor others, which helps them in their career path. People can make a career with a manager who motivates them to learn. Graduating from a school and possessing a degree only gives you entry into the organization. It is your responsibility to go from there, to climb the ladder through learning with different channels. Learning is the baseline for achieving your personal and organizational goals. In your personal life, you create a vision for your life. In order to realize your dream, you have to take different steps to move you forward. You have to create a road map and follow it.

Learning is at the heart of life. It is an integral part of life. When I talk about learning in this book, it is specifically for leaders who run a company, community, or country. Leaders have to be knowledgeable experts in their field. In order to boost your economy, you need to encourage economists to learn new skills and utilize them.

Conclusion

It is of paramount importance for leaders to continuously learn new skills in order to cope with challenges in a volatile environment. Learning is key to a leader's success; it converts followers into leaders and leaders into change agents. Learning is an integral part of the career path for leaders. They inspire every member of the organization to learn and develop. Learning prepares you for every challenge. An organization is a learning company where everyone finds a career path by learning continuously. Training is arranged for workers. Effective leaders are learners and create a culture of learning. Organizations and institutions that don't remain static are successful and dynamic; they adapt to the changing environment with a learning culture. It is your learning that brought you to your leadership position. With learning, you are not in a static position; you continuously move on. Adapting to environmental challenges keeps you alert. Leaders as learners succeed in difficult situations when others fail. In every failure or setback, they find an opportunity and learning lesson.

Leaders should be well informed all the time. They create a team of professionals who transform the organization and give it an outstanding reputation. They are role models and are known in the market and the community. All entrepreneurs have to keep in mind that the foundation of any business is based on continuous learning. Learning is not only for the sake of learning, but it has to be implemented. There must be a system of knowledge management that is accessible to everyone in the organization.

Bibliography

"5 Reasons Why All Leaders Are Readers." https://magazine.startus.cc. Accessed 15 Dec. 2020.

Adair, J. (1998). *Effective Leadership: How to Develop Leadership Skills.* London: Macmillan.

Boutros-Ghali, B., et al. (1998). *Essays on Leadership.* New York: Carnegie Corporation.

Covey, S. R. (1992). *Principle-Centered Leadership.* New York: Simon & Schuster.

Covey, S. R. (2004). *The 7 Habits of Highly Effective People: Powerful Lessons in Personal Change. Restoring the Character Ethic.* New York: Simon & Schuster.

https://www.thehrdirector.com/features/leadership/leader-coach-affecting-organisational-success-growth-place-curiosity-empathy/. Accessed 15 Dec. 2020.

CHAPTER 9

Charismatic Leaders

CHARISMATIC LEADERS HAVE COMPELLING ATTRACTIVENESS and charm that can inspire devotion in others. Charisma is 50 per cent innate and 50 per cent learned. Charisma attracts people to follow you. Charismatic leaders are confident and are always in self-control. They are optimistic and see the glass as half-full instead of half-empty. Charismatic leaders have the following qualities: confidence, creativity, vision, determination, and communication.

Followers need aspirations and goals. Followers submit to the leader's vision, which inspires them to realize their own goals. Charismatic leaders are also known as transformational leaders but there is a little difference. Charismatic leaders improve the status quo while transformational leaders transform the organization into a leader's vision. Charismatic leaders influence and inspire people to achieve goals set by the leader. They have strong written and verbal communication skills. They address the emotions of the people. Charismatic leaders are role models and share their clear vision. They are not satisfied with the status quo and try to improve it. Their vision is understood by followers; they motivate them and get their commitment to enact change.

They are hard workers and think more about others than themselves. They are good speakers and self-aware. They have empathy for others and guide their followers on how to achieve corporate goals. They transfer confidence to their followers. People are happy working with them and are inspired to achieve their own goals. People don't feel isolated and are engaged in their mission. Everyone is highly committed and works hard. They are not controlled and work independently in a free atmosphere. They get a reputation for their style. They help people rise out of poverty to self-sufficiency. They do not force people to get commitment. Charismatic leaders and followers have a common goal.

Their struggle and dedication are for one common goal. They work day and night to achieve the goals of common interest. They are selfless and expend their energy for the betterment of the people. They communicate to others with heart, motivate them, and inspire them.

It is of paramount importance for leaders to be charismatic and attract followers. Political leaders and organizational leaders stand out if they are charismatic. Charismatic leaders have the following qualities that others don't have:

Self-confidence and self-belief: Charismatic leaders are self-confident and believe in themselves. Confidence is a key quality in leaders. In all situations, they are self-confident and decisive. They know what to do and when. They believe in themselves and in their vision; they know they will realize it. They deliver what they say. They have no fear of failure. Obstacles don't obstruct them; they instruct them, and they know which course to take and when. They persevere and are persistent until they realize their dream into reality. They are charming and appealing to the public. They use their charisma for the public interest and serve them with all their capabilities. They deliver influential speeches and inspire their followers to achieve corporate objectives. Their charisma gets people to commit to change. They are free to act when they see it's the right time. Leaders create a friendly environment for followers. They transfer their values to others. They coach their followers and create new leaders.

Inspirational: This is another key quality of charismatic leaders. They inspire followers to move forward to achieve corporate goals. They communicate their vision to followers, verbally and written. They energize people to work hard and go forward on the path they chose. Followers are motivated and enjoy working cohesively.

Dynamic: Charismatic leaders are very dynamic. They are enthusiastic, share new ideas about the business, and continuously think of changes needed to keep up with the time. They keep an eye on the market, political situation, and government regulations, and they adapt the organization to new realities. They never procrastinate. They move forward with key solutions for the business. They are very effective, competent, and disciplined. They monitor themselves in all situations. They accept positive and negative feedback, and change their behaviour if necessary. They are self-aware and know their strengths and weaknesses. They are emotionally intelligent, adjust their behaviour if necessary, and try to be in self-control (see chapter 5 for more details). They are not controlled by others and decide their own destinies. They are mature, proactive, and decisive. They know when to act, based on circumstances, and avoid careless or immature actions. They don't regret what they do and can justify their decisions. They think a lot, see the situation from all angles, consult their team, listen to feedback from others, and make decisions acceptable to everyone.

Charismatic leaders have a positive body language. Their smiling faces attract people. Their body language is in line with their words, and they don't hide things. They are accessible to their people. They give their ideas and want to see the organization improve. They use technology and modern techniques to replace old systems and promote change.

Charismatic leaders represent their organization, and their personality reflects the company, which is known for its behaviour, values, and principles. Their values are the company's values. They display ethical behaviour, integrity, fairness, and honesty. They play an important role in the popularity of the organization; for example, Gianni Agnelli represents Fiat in Italy, Bill Gates represents Microsoft, and so on. Charismatic leaders find creative ways to solve problems. People are encouraged to be creative and find new ways to do their job. The company is not a box where people are forced to use one method. Charismatic leaders encourage new ideas and new solutions to problems. All team members are creative when faced with new challenges. They use new methods to cope with complex issues and expected disasters. This results in organizational development. They also have compassion and feel the suffering of others.

Charismatic national leaders take action when people are affected by natural disasters like earthquakes and floods. They mobilize their people to help those affected. Charismatic leaders don't remain silent when they see people suffering; they use all their resources to help them and pull them out of a disastrous situation. Their followers also take the same path. Inspiring leaders leave a legacy for others to follow. They listen to others and keep eye contact when speaking to them. They don't want to be distracted when listening to colleagues, friends, and others. They often take notes while listening. Some leaders don't have good listening skills and forget whatever people tell them. They pretend they are listening, but their mind is elsewhere during the conversation. Charismatic leaders stand out in listening power. They make people feel they have been heard. They listen and reflect and take action and give feedback to people. This is a great skill that is learned.

Outstanding charismatic leaders have the following qualities:

1. Personal attention: They have empathy with others and give them personal attention. They meet everyone, listen to them, and accept their ideas. They don't ignore people's concerns. They are not limited to their circle but consider the feelings of others. They don't make decisions without listening to others. They get the consensus of others before making big decisions.

2. Energy: They motivate and energize others to give outstanding results. They are inspired to move up and perform at a higher level. They use all their capacity with modern techniques to boost production/output and do above-average work. They don't waste time or resources.

3. Sociable: They live a social life and have empathy for others. They are sensitive to other's worries. They react with sympathy to their emotions. They talk to them and try to relieve their stress by sharing their feelings with them. This is the key quality of a charismatic

leader. They are loved by others because of their attitude towards them. When someone has a trauma, they quickly react.

4. Communications: They are good communicators and share their vision with others very clearly. They are eloquent and good speakers. Their language is very clear. They communicate to everyone. They transmit their plans, strategies, goals, and objectives to all team members. They get feedback from others. They create a culture where communication is encouraged. Communication plays an important role in the development of an organization.

5. Homogenous teams: Inspiring and charismatic leaders build well-integrated teams who work for a common goal. Members help and support each other and act in a cohesive manner. Leaders produce team members who continuously try to improve their work. They believe that teams produce more than individuals working separately. Teams are coached and well equipped with knowledge and skills to cope with different types of problems. Leaders continuously monitor the teams, and they ensure the contribution of the teams towards corporate objectives. Charismatic leaders keep an eye on group leaders and communicate with them about day-to-day updates and strategy change.

6. Self-development: Charismatic leaders are always concerned for self-development and improvement; they always monitor themselves. They go to training, get feedback from peers and others, and work on self-development. They learn all types of skills necessary to run a business and lead the organization to realize their dreams and visions. They are also regarded as transformational leaders, although there is a difference between the two. The concern and objective of both are to move forward and develop the organization and give it a better position. Transformational leaders make radical changes to transform the organization. On the other hand, charismatic leaders are not happy with the status quo; they reengineer processes and make other changes to meet contemporary needs. They want to see the organization in

better shape. Charismatic leaders are transformational, but not all transformational leaders are charismatic. Charismatic leaders change the lives of people and prepare them for all challenges. They are equipped with knowledge and skills to solve any problem. When faced with a problem, charismatic leaders try to solve it and see it as an opportunity to learn. Problems give them lessons to find novel solutions. They address it proactively and avoid it in the future. They give them new opportunities.

Charismatic leaders are capable of reading people's body language. They also understand and observe the mood of individuals. When they give a speech, they assess the mood of the audience and accordingly deliver their speech. They don't work on their own agenda but do what is in the best interest of the people. They are proactive and sensitive to surroundings and aware of the environment and react quickly to any changes. They take care of people's health and avoid pollution. They also keep an eye on political changes and adapt their organization to new demands and needs.

7. Self-confidence: This is a key quality of charismatic leaders. They are self-confident and believe in themselve. They have vision and believe they can realize it. They imagine their dream and use all resources and efforts to realize it. They are never disappointed or discouraged by the fear of failure. They have a strong commitment to their vision, which they see in the future. They also convince others to believe in themselves and get their commitment to achieving goals. They focus on the outcome and want to see goals achieved. They are not worried about too many activities. Every team member is expected to give the desired results. Corporate strategies determine what results are expected from teams and individuals.

8. Delegation: Leaders coach, delegate, and empower others to do their jobs. They produce skilled professionals. They trust them and encourage them for their achievements. They admire team

members and give them a sense of confidence and energy. The empowerment increases the productivity of individuals, who work freely and with confidence. They do not deskill others; instead, they use their full potential. They build the capacity of their followers to face challenges. They build teams which are well known for performance, dedication, quality, integrity, cohesiveness, commitment, and hard work. Equipped with such qualities, they create an unchallengeable position for them. They have an outstanding position in society as leaders. They feel honoured for belonging to the group. This attracts others to join them.

9. Persistence: Charismatic leaders never give up. They are persistent, they persevere, and they are not afraid of challenges and obstacles. Obstacles give them lessons and instructions. They keep their dream in mind. They have a target and act to reach it, whatever it takes. Whatever the circumstances are, they move forward with their team. They don't wait for an ideal situation. They are not worried about bad weather. They imagine their dream and see it being achieved.

10. Determination: Leaders have a strong determination and keep moving forward. They are not worried about negative feedback. They work day and night, and are very resourceful. They gather all resources that contribute to achieving their corporate goals. They are highly committed to their ideological goals. They stick to their ideology. Nelson Mandela once said, "If a leader changes his ideology, he is not a leader." The key goal of leaders is to work on their ideology, which translates into their vision for the betterment of the people. Their ideology is based on a change in the way of life. They are not happy with the status quo and take into view the faults of the current system. They keep their ideology on the top and work day and night to achieve their ideological goals. They focus on the future and see it differently. They act for future goals. They have long-term and short-term goals which contribute to their vision. They evaluate their progress from time to time and ensure that everything is going as planned.

11. Charisma: Political leaders learn charisma to attract the public. They train themselves with deliberate charisma to appeal to the public and get their commitment for achieving goals. Charisma is learned through practice. They use a style imitating charismatic leaders. Charismatic leaders are storytellers. They start with a story which supports their argument and get the attention of the audience. Storytelling is used by charismatic leaders in every public speech.

12. Humility: Charismatic leaders are humble. They are not proud or arrogant. They have good relations with people, serve others, and keep their profile low. They are like a magnet and attract others with their charm. As it is said that success is mostly relational. You get success by having good friends, colleagues, and peers who contribute to your success. You attract people with the same values you have.

13. The law of attraction: As the law says that like attracts like. A charismatic leader attracts people who have the same ideas, goals, and mission. According to Brian Tracy, a motivational speaker, "You attract those who are in harmony to your thoughts." Charismatic leaders have a positive attitude and are optimistic. Their thoughts are always about success, development, improvement, and the welfare of others. They release negative thoughts and develop positive energy in others. They give hope to others. They create a culture where everyone is self-motivated, and people with negative thoughts don't exist. They coach, develop, and promote others; there is no barrier to success. Everyone is treated fairly, and people climb the ladder only on a merit basis; there is fairness and transparency. They create homogeneous groups with the same values. According to Tracy, charisma is perception. Charismatic leaders work on their perception and create a good impression in the eyes of others. They speak to the hearts of the people.

Conclusion

Charismatic leaders have charm and attract others and get their commitment. They inspire others with their charisma. They get others to make commitments. Charismatic leaders are confident and under control. They don't micromanage. Charismatic leaders are creative and innovative; they find new ways to achieve their goals. They have a lot of determination. They have good communication skills. They have high integrity.

Charismatic leaders change the lives of others. Organizations, communities, and countries need a charismatic leader to bring change. One can work on charisma, to create and develop it. Nations develop leaders who are selfless, dedicated, efficient, and charismatic.

Bibliography

Adair, J. (1998). *Effective Leadership: How to Develop Leadership Skills*. London: Macmillan.

Boutros-Ghali, B., et al. (1998). *Essays on Leadership*. New York: Carnegie Corporation.

Covey, S. R. (1992). *Principle-Centered Leadership*. New York: Simon & Schuster.

Covey, S. R. (2004). *The 7 Habits of Highly Effective People: Powerful Lessons in Personal Change. Restoring the Character Ethic*. New York: Simon & Schuster.

https://www.psychologytoday.com/ us/blog/cutting-edge-leadership.

https://www.researchgate.net/ publication/322039088_Charismatic_ Leadership.

CHAPTER 10

Transformational Leaders and Model Leaders

A TRANSFORMATIONAL LEADER IS THE one who encourages, inspires, and motivates others to create change. They empower others to work for the interest of the group, sacrificing their own interest. They are role models for such actions. Their key theme is to transform the organization, community, or country for the betterment of the people. The key qualities of transformational leaders are as follows:-

1. They point out the need for change. Transformational leaders work with their team to identify the need for change. The shortcomings of the current system are studied and noted. Leaders give a new vision for a better future.

2. They develop a vision and a strategy to achieve it. They then develop the vision, which promises a better future. They develop a strategy and road map to realize their dream. There is a structured strategy that has to be implemented to achieve corporate goals. The strategy will be in the line with the culture of the organization, people's behaviour, and the needs of the group.

3. They lead the change with motivation. Transformational leaders lead the change by inspiring and motivating people. They work

in a holistic manner with mutual collaboration to achieve the corporate goals, and they see a better life in the change. Leaders take risks and guide people till the end. They make sure that all individuals contribute to it. They coach and mentor people to accept higher responsibilities. Transformational leaders develop individuals and create other leaders with high performance. They transform the organization and people to perform above the existing level. They empower others and produce new leaders and create self-efficiency in others. They independently work with full capacity to give excellent results. They don't micromanage, which demoralizes people. They sacrifice their own interests and work for the betterment of others. They work as servants of others. They also create values in the followers who work selflessly for the group. They innovate and create change.

4. They are intellectual role models. Transformational leaders are intellectual and well equipped with knowledge. They are well aware of what is required. They are also proactive and well disciplined. As role models, they set their example, and others follow them. In today's changing world, with Volatility, Uncertainty, Complexity, and Ambiguity (VUCA), transformational leaders are needed to change organizations and corporations, putting them on the right path. They create a culture where people are skilled and well equipped with knowledge and expertise to handle VUCA and adapt quickly to a changing environment. They have a planned and systematic approach to change. They increase the potential of staff, who improve and produce better results. They attract, retain, develop, and engage people. They are the driving force of transformation. They build the capacity of people to achieve greater effectiveness. They assess an organization, its culture, people's behaviour, and values, and devise a strategy for change. They organize training for those who will lead change and those affected by the transformation. They carefully evaluate the need of the organization and its viability. They consider it from all angles and then take appropriate action.

Transformation may result in mergers, acquisitions, or outsourcing. Effective transformation depends on the ability of leader. Transformational leaders create teams with professional and skilled members. They focus on results. Their vision attracts people with high commitment. They are imaginative, flexible, accessible, and supportive. They give feedback to team members whenever necessary and keep them on the right path. Transformational leaders have a responsible position. They need to have the authority to bring change. As executives of an organization, they can lead the transformation. They not only share their vision but also present a compelling mission that gives the organization a purpose or reason for existence. They are ethical and have a positive impact on people. They have morals and earn the people's trust. Their ethics, morality, and honesty have a greater influence on people than authority. They are team focussed and facilitate collaboration to emphasize vision. They are emotionally intelligent and quickly react to the emotions of others.

Transformational leaders are found in political groups, educational institutions, financial organizations, technology, entertainment, and other areas. Transformational leaders are bold and take action without hesitation, in consensus with the team. They not only transform the system and organization but also transform the people. They create momentum in followers with their vision. They develop their followers to take higher responsibilities and face new challenges. They create intellectual followers and equip them with knowledge and skills. They are adventurous and find new ways to realize their vision. They are risk-takers. Their vision attracts everyone, and the whole team is dedicated to achieving the desired goals and results. They have a powerful influence on others with their honesty, empathy, authenticity, hard work, commitment, and dedication. They engage their people, and everyone feels a sense of involvement in decision-making. They consider everyone individually, talk to them, and listen to their views about any issue. They respect the opinions of others and consider them during decision-making. They identify challenges, discuss them with the team, give their opinion, and also get the opinion of others.

Transformational leaders have to accept where they are and formulate a strategy and road map to take them to their final destination. If there is any ambiguity, misunderstanding, or uncertainty in the team, the transformational leader controls the situation and reenergizes the members. Good leaders can control any situation and keep followers moving forward. Transformational leaders are enthusiastic, passionate, and energetic. They are supportive, genuine, and trustworthy, and they want positive change for people. They care about the people's well-being. They inspire others to be change agents and never give up. Transformational leaders are highly effective and shake up the organization, community, or country. To be a transformational leader, you have to get rid of traditional and conventional ways, which may be a barrier to your vision of transforming the organization.

Transformational leaders give their lives to the organization and the people working there. Under transformational leaders, people are very happy and motivated as compared to other leaders. They feel secure and self-motivated. They keep high morale of his followers. Such leaders encourage satisfaction. They face problems and issues, and try to solve them. Transformational leaders are happy to find solutions with the help of the team. Good leaders want to hear about problems, so they can solve them. Bill Gates once said, "I am happy to receive bad news. If I don't like it, people won't tell me, and that will be the beginning of the end."

Transformational leaders are facilitators. They facilitate the work of the people and keep them going. They keep an eye on the progress. They have organizational skills. They are highly disciplined. They mobilize people to a common goal, and everyone gives his contribution. They avoid unnecessary activities that don't contribute to their vision and organizational goals. They pick up key tasks and prioritize them by value. They use the 20/80 rule (they work on 20 per cent of tasks that give 80 per cent of results). They have a strong set of values and a sense of mission and give a purpose to the organization. They come up with good ideas through brainstorming.

Transformational leaders are lifelong learners. They learn from every situation and challenge. They persevere in conflicts and convince opponents that transformation will change their lives. They involve their team members in discussions about transformation and also talk to other stakeholders like donors, board members, and so on. Transformational leaders explain to everyone that change is inevitable. This is the only way to solve problems and live a better life. New realities in the market, new political developments, and environmental changes oblige organizations to transform.

Change can be positive. Transformational leaders challenge long-held perception and assumption; they also change perceptions. They work day and night to move forward. They believe that team output is greater than the sum of the individuals at work. Teams not only give better results but also give good ideas.

Transformational leaders integrate operational and technological teams. Instead of competition, they collaborate and give fantastic results. They consume full energy to give better results, achieve team objectives, and contribute to corporate goals. This also enhances their personal development and paves the way for their career path. New transformational leaders are produced who take responsibility. They create a culture that encourages development. The organization expands in a few years and the number of people increases.

Transformational leaders translate strategies into action. They are action-oriented. They not only support their followers but also produce the resources required for the job. They share their vision and create a strong network of loyal people. Transformational political leaders communicate their vision to everyone. They study the needs of the people, their concerns, and their worries about the future. They consider all this and then develop a vision and strategy. They deliver speeches to thousands of people, communicating their vision for the nation. They are ready to accept any failure or setback, and continue their journey towards the ultimate goal. They remove barriers and encourage independent thinking. They internalize moral standards and display self-regulated, self-imposed behaviour. They never bargain on their principles. They keep themselves on the frontline, and others follow them; this is what leaders should do.

Transformational leaders are the first to take action and then coach others to follow the same direction. They share their knowledge and skills with their team. They model the way for the team. They leverage their emotional intelligence, listen to others, and share their worries and concerns. They engage their talented people to their fullest capacity.

They build strategic relationships with others to achieve organizational goals. The use all their skills for the benefit of the organization and don't pursue their own interests. They speak to the hearts of the people. They are persuasive and build commitment to their vision among the people. They inspire followers to move forward.

Transformational leaders are very transparent. They don't hide anything. Everyone can see what is happening in the organization. They inspire and motivate others to manage risks and face challenges. Risk management is necessary to move forward. They proactively address the risks involved in operations and prepare the team to mitigate them. Model leaders are role models for public responsibility. They set examples for their followers. This is because of the high performance of the people they lead.

Performance is measured inside and outside the organization. There are continuous evaluations of performance, and any deviations from the target are addressed. They establish key performance indicators for the team. They focus on outcomes and results. They make partnerships with internal and external stakeholders, and build good relationships with suppliers and clients. In times of need, they know who is who and get information from the right person. They are well informed and updated due to their strong relationships with others.

They are focussed on customers and keep them first. They take surveys and circulate questionnaires and use other means to know customers' opinions; this keeps the organization customer-oriented. They are concerned about the environment and also about the social and economic betterment of the community. They are holistic thinkers and integrate cross-functions in the organization. Units are integrated and tackle issues in a cohesive manner. They create knowledge in the organization and make it accessible to everyone. They remove ambiguity and uncertainty after someone departs. Model leaders are well respected and have integrity. They are the servants of their followers. They create a culture of service. People in a time of need or disaster look to leaders and their actions. Model leaders are proactive and reach the people and mobilize their resources.

Types of Leaders

There are several types of leaders:

1. Charismatic: This type of leadership is very effective. Such leaders have charm; they attract followers, get their commitment, energize them, and inspire them.

2. Democratic: These leaders ask others for their opinion. They don't make decisions without the consensus of others. The decision is taken in consultation with team members.

3. Transactional: Transactional leaders follow the chain of command. They use the approach of the carrot and the stick. They reward people for good performance and penalize them for bad performance.

4. Situational: These leaders use different approaches, depending on the situation. They use the style that's appropriate for the specific moment.

5. Servant: These leaders encourage collective decision-making and power-sharing. They are called the servants of their followers. People are highly committed to such leaders. These leaders are very effective and always help the people. They are well aware of the people's concerns and are available for help.

6. Transformational: This type was explained earlier in this chapter.

7. Autocratic: These leaders exert significant control over the organization. They rarely accept the suggestions of others. They don't share power. These leaders are not very effective. They create uncertainty in their followers. Power rests in the hands of one person.

8. Bureaucratic: These leaders work in highly regulated environments with strict adherence to rules and regulations. They are not very effective. They rarely use their judgment.

9. Laissez-faire: This is a French phrase that means "let them do." These leaders allow the staff to do the job as they see fit. They delegate authority to subordinates. They rarely involve themselves in their job. These leaders are not very effective. They are unaware of daily tasks. They don't coach others, which results in a lack of development. Inexperienced people make bad decisions.

10. Ethical: These leaders are honest and have strong values and principles. Ethics is the key ingredient for these leaders. Ethical leaders are very effective and highly respected. The majority of leaders work for the interests of someone. All types of leader should be honest.

Leadership Examples

There are many examples throughout history, but I have taken only one who is very famous for serving his nations: Nelson Mandela of South Africa.

Nelson Mandela was the most important political leader in South Africa. He was one of the greatest politicians in the world. He is well known and liked across the world. He served as president of South Africa from 1994 to 1999. In 1993, he was awarded the Noble Peace Price for ending the system of racial segregation known as apartheid in South Africa. He laid the foundation of democracy in South Africa. He treated all the people equally and fairly. He was born on 18 July 1918 in Mvezi, Transkei region, in South Africa. His father was Gadla Henry Mphakanyiswa of Tembu tribe. Mandela studied law at the University of Fort Hare.

In 1944, he played a leading role in the creation of the African National Congress (ANC). The party aimed to end racial discrimination against the African majority. In 1948, racial segregation began. Mandela was arrested in 1952. He was also tried for treason between 1956 and 1962 but was cleared.

The ANC was outlawed by the government in 1960, after the Sharpeville massacre.

In 1962, Mandela was again arrested for organizing a demonstration and leaving the country without authorization. He was sentenced to five years. He was then tried for involvement in a plot to forcibly overthrow the government, and on 12 June 1964, he was sentenced to life imprisonment. He remained in jail for twenty-seven years, and during this period, his popularity increased. The prison made him a symbol of resistance and a martyr in the fight against racism. In 1982, he was moved to a high-security prison. He did not compromise on his mission and refused offers of freedom.

On 11 February 1990, after twenty-seven years in jail, Mandela was released. He became president of the ANC in 1991. At that point, a historic meeting with de Klerk led the two leaders to realize that only a compromise between white and black people would prevent a civil war in South Africa. In late 1991, the Convention for a Democratic South Africa (CODESA) was established with the aim of creating a new government elected by all citizens.

South Africa held its first democratic elections on 27 April 1994. The ANC won with 62 per cent of votes, and Mandela became president. De Klerk's party, which gained 20 per cent of votes, was included in the first national unity government. During his presidency, Mandela worked to maintain peace and to boost the country's economy. He favoured forgiveness to vengeance and demonstrated it by creating the Truth and Reconciliation Commission in 1995. Even those who committed abuse and violence during the apartheid regime were cleared.

Nelson Mandela quit political life in 1999, leaving to Vice President Thabo Mbeki the task of continuing his path. Mandela passed away in Johannesburg on 5 December 2013.

Bibliography

Adair, J. (1998). *Effective Leadership: How to Develop Leadership Skills.* London: Macmillan.

Boutros-Ghali, B., et al. (1998). *Essays on Leadership.* New York: Carnegie Corporation.

Covey, S. R. (1992). *Principle-Centered Leadership.* New York: Simon & Schuster.

Covey, S. R. (2004). *The 7 Habits of Highly Effective People: Powerful Lessons in Personal Change. Restoring the Character Ethic.* New York: Simon & Schuster.

https://www.bbc.co.uk/history/historic_figures/ /jinnah_mohammad_ali.shtml;

https://www.britannica.com/ "biography/Mohammed Ali Jinnah" | Pakistani governor-general Britannica;

https://www.biography.com/political-figure/muhammad-ali-jinnah.

https://www.biographyonline.net/politicians/nelson-mandela.html.

CHAPTER 11

Covid-19: A Challenge for Leaders

COVID-19 IS A NEW CORONAVIRUS that was reported in Wuhan, China, in 2019. Covid-19 is an infectious disease that can spread from person to person. It has spread all over the world. The symptoms can range from mild to severe illness. One can become infected by close contact with others. Old people are at high risk. Staying home most of the time and keeping a mandatory distance is the only way to avoid contacting the virus.

It was originally found in China, but as people travelled abroad, they took the virus with them, and it quickly spread to Europe and North America. In Italy, it hit Lombardia province, where hundreds of people died. The Italian authorities were very quick to announce a lockdown and told people to stay home and maintain social distancing when going out for necessities. Bars, restaurants, and schools were closed.

Other countries followed Italy in locking down. The virus hit Brazil, India, Pakistan, and other countries. In March 2020, the World Health Organization (WHO) declared it pandemic. WHO issued instructions for safety. People were advised to wear masks when going out, wash their hands with sanitizer, and keep at least one metre (six feet) away from others. Public gatherings were banned in most countries. Churches and mosques were closed.

Some Covid-19 statistics from WHO, as of 28 March 2021:

Total confirmed cases globally   126,119,639

Deaths   2,766,831

Poor people were severely affected by the lockdown, especially in poor countries, where people depended on their daily earnings. It had a huge effect on business worldwide. This is a big challenge to government institutions, corporations, and organizations. Organizations have to reinvent themselves. People are forced to work from home. Although it has affected business tremendously, many organizations survived with new challenges. The Internet has played a big role and facilitated the jobs of organizations, corporations, and government bodies. If this had happened thirty years ago, before the Internet and mobile phones were widespread, it would have destroyed the world.

The private sector also faced severe losses. Air travel came to a halt due to a travel ban. Airlines cut their workforce significantly. Hotel rooms were empty. People started working remotely from their homes. Meetings were held online through Zoom and Skype. Digital signatures were accepted through business transactions. Although there was a big loss, big players continued their business. People learned new skills during this challenge. Leaders with democratic styles were successful. Employees worked even harder from home.

This was also a big challenge for political leaders. Unemployment rose considerably in some countries. Leaders had to face that and find a way out. Some companies went bankrupt. There was no contingency plan. People were not prepared to work from home.

Isolation also affected people emotionally. People went through depression due to loneliness. Hospitals were full of patients. Booking for doctor visits and check-ups was discontinued. This had an enormous effect on patients with other diseases. People had few facilities to work from home. Leaders need to have empathy with everyone whether they are staff members or not. CEOs have to show themselves as members of society and help people at this critical moment. This is a humanitarian crisis, and everyone must contribute. Some people lost their jobs and have nothing to do. They deserve help from rich people. They need to be given jobs.

As a result of Covid-19, Internet use has increased. People use social media more than before. Online sales have also increased. Some people cannot go to the supermarket, so they order supplies online. Purchases through Amazon increased. Some companies reopened after lockdown with limited staff. Face-to-face meetings have been discontinued; only online meetings are allowed. Organizations with people from different countries allow their staff to work from home. Working from home has other advantages. People don't spend time on travel from home to the office and back from the office to home. Another advantage of working from home is that you are more concentrated and focussed on your task. In the office, you may be distracted from time to time and socialize with people.

But there are also problems. With no social interaction with colleagues, you depend on email and Skype. Staying at home and not exercising can cause health problems, like weight gain.

Women with children face problems when working from home. They face distractions all the time. With schools closed, children are at home. It is the parents' responsibility to take care of them. Some schools and universities reopened but closed again when Covid-19 affected the teachers. National and global leaders are under tremendous pressure due to economic crises. This is a new scenario for them, and they are trying their best to overcome it.

There are food crises. The pandemic also affected already displaced people in refugee camps; for example, thousands of Syrian refugees in Turkey were severely affected. They also faced Covid-19 symptoms due to inadequate medical facilities. In this critical moment, leaders have to come up with full resources and should have empathy with victims. They should show a sense of responsibility for the people around them. They have to show themselves in a visible manner and reach out to all.

Leaders have to make people feel confident. People are worried about their jobs and future. Leaders have to take steps to save their people. They are working hard in unfavourable conditions. They have to encourage them that their work is important and they have the full support of the leader. National leaders have to take steps necessary to save the lives of the people. They have to open medical centres and take precautions to protect people from this coronavirus. WHO has given instructions to every country to advise their people. Leaders have to ensure a lockdown to avoid spreading the disease. They have to ensure that the business continuity is not affected. People's jobs should be secured. Leaders have to worry about the economy and ensure stability. Traders should be encouraged to continue exports. Opportunists take advantage of such a situation and make stocks of basic commodities, hide them from the market, and increase the prices. Leaders have to ensure that basic commodities are available in the market at a reasonable price.

This is a once-in-a-century event that has affected people all over the world; leaders have to handle it unanimously and help each other. Covid-19 has also affected the mental health of the people. Leaders have to keep a contingency plan in place to tackle the situation. We still don't know what the long-term economic and social effects of this pandemic will be. Small and large businesses have moved to virtual working. Some small businesses were not prepared for such situations and had tremendous problems. Big organizations and corporations where virtual working is normal were not affected that much. Employee performance didn't change.

In the education sector, leaders arranged virtual teaching. Students continued their studies through virtual lessons without going to school in person. Education in developed countries was not affected that much. In developing countries, education was highly affected. Many children remained at home without education. This pandemic has affected all spheres of life. People are not allowed to take part in public ceremonies. In some countries, people are not allowed to visit relatives or gather in friends' homes. It has created a social vacuum. Children staying at home feel lonely. They go to parks and other areas but miss their friends and do not have other children to play with.

Covid-19 has also had environmental effects. Petrol consumption has decreased considerably, which has resulted in a reduction of pollution. Pollution in big cities like London and New York decreased considerably, resulting in cleaner air. The aviation sector was also severely affected, as international travel dropped significantly.

Some countries like Germany and New Zealand responded effectively to Covid-19. These countries took proactive measures. In mid-March, Germany closed schools and retail businesses and did more than 100,000 coronavirus tests per week. New Zealand announced a total lockdown on 23 March and controlled the spread of the disease to a large extent.

The following qualities are needed for leaders during this pandemic.

- Be empathetic and think about employees, customers, and clients. Keep your objective first and try to find opportunities.
- Be quick in decision-making.
- Stick to your compelling vision.
- Take a long-term view of the situation.

Covid-19 is a social, economic, and political crisis, apart from a health crisis. It has challenged economists, sociologists, and politicians. It has brought misery to millions worldwide. People are indoors with a lack of economic activity. It is a leadership crisis. It tests leaders. Self-interest is at the centre of organizational behaviour. Businesses exist to create profits for shareholders. Leaders have hard choices. They have to keep the mission in their minds but have also to demonstrate social behaviour and empathy. With all this uncertainty, you don't know what will happen tomorrow. Leaders have to be transparent and reachable in such a situation. The key thing is that leaders have to be honest with the organization, shareholders, and other stakeholders. They have to work hard with their hearts and heads. They have to know how to lead and act in critical moments. They have to lead. They have to know their priorities, goals, strengths, and weaknesses. Leaders have to know how to conduct themselves in a changing environment and adapt to it.

There is a strategic shift. Leaders have to find game-changing solutions for their problems. Before, they could hold meetings in an office. Now, this has changed, and they are holding meetings remotely through Skype, Zoom, and so on. This is a great shift, and they have to ensure the health of their business and have to be resourceful.

This is a historic moment to reflect on your goals. It is a moment to look inside, discover yourself, and see if your values are in line with your work. Have you given up your dreams? This moment can change us forever.

Leadership is an unending journey. You continuously change and improve yourself. With new challenges, you learn more and more. This prepares you for the future, and you will learn how to respond if this happens again. You will become strong enough to face any unexpected challenges. You have to create your network and advance your goals. You have to be resilient. Take people in your confidence. Be in continuous communication with your staff, and reassure them that leadership is doing their best to meet their needs, now and in the future. You have to reach out to everyone. You have to see new opportunities in this situation.

Conclusion

Covid-19 is an unprecedented pandemic that has affected the whole world. So far, it has spread to 216 countries. It's taken the lives of millions of people and spread very quickly across the globe. People are obliged to work remotely from home. The global economy has been adversely affected. Many businesses closed, resulting in unemployment. This is a humanitarian crisis and has to be coped with together. It is like pollution, which doesn't stay within your borders. This is a challenge and a test for leaders. They have to demonstrate their ability to cope with it. They have to be patient and persistent to save people's health and repair the economy.

References

Adair, J. (1998). *Effective Leadership: How to Develop Leadership Skills*. London: Macmillan.

Boutros-Ghali, B., et al. (1998). *Essays on Leadership*. New York: Carnegie Corporation.

Covey, S. R. (1992). *Principle-Centered Leadership*. New York: Simon & Schuster.

Covey, S. R. (2004). *The 7 Habits of Highly Effective People: Powerful Lessons in Personal Change. Restoring the Character Ethic.* New York: Simon & Schuster.

https://360.here.com/covid-19-impact-traffic-congestion.

https://www.bing.com/videos/search.

https://www.cdc.gov/coronavirus/2019-ncov/downloads/2019-ncov-factsheet.pdf.

https://www.mckinsey.com/business-functions/risk/our-insights/covid-19-implications-for-business.

http://www.ila-net.org/Reflections/dtourish.html?gclid=EAIaIQobChMI7fmphane7AIVhxh7Ch2InA.

https://theconversation.com/how-leadership-in-various-countries-has-affected-covid-19-response-effectiveness-138692.

https://hbswk.hbs.edu/item/18-tips-managers-can-use-to-navigate-covid-s-rising-waters

https://www.worldometers.info/coronavirus/.

https://covid19.who.int/.